# Turtle

Published by Turtle

turtle.global

Paperback ISBN: 987-1-7376332-1-1

1. SOC00200 | SOCIAL SCIENCE / Anthropology General

2. NAT011000 | NATURE / Environmental Conservation and Protection

3. PSY053000 | PSYCHOLOGY / Evolutionary Psychology

First Edition

# Contents

Expanded Contents                                    1

1.  Perceptive Perspective                          18

2.  Mind My Brain                                   40

3.  Leaving the Path I'm on Behind                  55

4.  Finding Time to Find Me                        114

5.  Our Species and the Faults We Possess          140

6.  The Young of Our Species                       225

# Expanded Contents

**Chapter 1: Perceptive Perspective** – *page 17*

1.1 The answers to all of my problems are all around me

1.2 My cowardly self

1.3 A conversation with me and myself

1.4 Genetically similar to others?

1.5 Genetic excuses for my life's problems.

1.6 Brain A versus Brain B/ Living as me in another time period

1.7 Superficial Intelligence/ Another conversation with myself

1.8 Repeated habits

1.9 Me and my bad sense of direction

1.10 Learning from a child

1.11 Learning how not to get lost

1.12 Finding my problems in me

1.13 Doing the opposite of what I wanted to do

- Looking at me and my problems from a different perspective


**Chapter 2: Mind My Brain** – *page 39*

2.1 Mind versus brain

2.2 Our brains as computers and our minds as filters

2.3 Inputting unbiased information

2.4 Forcing myself to do something different

2.5 Widening my perspective of myself

2.6 More questions to figure out

2.7 My jealousy of everyone and everything

- Finding a way to be comfortable with me

- Breakdowns of genetic versus environmental problems

2.8 Our powerful brain

2.9 Maximizing our Human intelligence


### Chapter 3: Leaving the Path I'm on Behind – *page 54*

3.1 Rebuilding/Rewiring my weak Human mind and not-so-intelligent brain

3.2 Converting my toxic, negative, obsessive mind into something that is not that

3.3 Productive tasks

3.4 Sustained success

3.5 Patterns of the successful and unsuccessful Humans

3.6 Reworking my physical space

3.7 The Greats going back to the basics

3.8 Rewiring my brain one shelf at a time

3.9 We have the Human Right to choose for ourselves

3.10 Figuring out my lifelong exercises

3.11 Finding my go-to exercise

3.12 My hatred of anything natural

3.13 Modern versus natural

3.14 Vibrations deep within us

3.15 Our cells remember

- Video game analogy of my life adventure

3.16 Back to our species' diet

- My percentage diet experimentation

3.17 My relationship with plants

3.18 Reshaping my life with new skills, more knowledge, and more variety

**Chapter 4: Finding Time to Find Me** – *page 113*

4.1 We all have the same 24 hours

4.2 How many wasted hours do I have each day, each week, each month

4.3 Unproductive time versus productive time

4.4 Would the 80- or 90-year old version of myself be content with the choices the younger me made?

4.5 Wasteful people wasting my time

4.6 A few minutes at a time

- Back to learning as a kid

4.7 The personality trait that I chose to work on first

- Lofty personal goals for my first decade of rebuilding my mind and my brain

4.8 Nine years after making my first Decade Goals list

- Managing our Forests like I manage my health

4.9 Taking any job

4.10 Music lessons

4.11 Hitting the music wall

4.12 Learning music without instruments

4.13 Humans and all of our exhausting self-made, life-inhibiting rules

4.14 Mastering many different areas of my life a little at a time

**Chapter 5: Our Species and the Faults We Possess** – *page 139*

5.1 Humans and other species

5.2 Three ways to build a Human brain

5.3 The hunted versus the unhunted

- The challenged versus the challenged

- Classroom A versus Classroom B

5.4 Is our species as "special" as we allow ourselves to think we are?

- Man-made Laws versus the Laws of Nature

5.5 The best and worst of our species

5.6 Generation after generation, year after year, same ole' Human Being

5.7 Variety, more than a "spice" of life?

5.8 Would we perform better as a species with high variety and diversity?

5.9 Defining a successful Human Being

5.10 The successful Humans

5.11 Accomplishing the incredible in the Netherlands

- Example of the Laws of Nature

5.12 The men during the Great Depression

5.13 Another one of our species' deeply woven thoughts/

- Examples of lower animals doing more complex things than many of our own species

5.14 Soldiers walking towards their death

5.15 Percentage of our species that influences my life decisions

- Standing up to those who hold me down

5.16 Are dealing with feelings and emotions that important?

- What's controlling our ability to feel?

5.17 Should we or should we not utilize our emotions?

5.18 The exhausting Human species. Another one of our species' faults

5.19 Obsessed with power and control

- Lines of control

5.20 What's the point of getting involved in other people's lives?

- Should I be telling others what to do with their own life?

- Letting stupid be stupid

5.21 More lines of controlled relationships

- Are we a young, naive, mistake-filled advanced species?

- The Universe's most powerful addiction?

5.22 From book clubs to hunting clubs, is our species the same chaotic mess?

5.23 Cleaning up my side of the street

- Rising above our species faults

5.24 Recognizing those Human mentalities that waste our time

- The patterns of those who control our lives

5.25 The family that ascended above the violence and inequality

5.26 Not being a victim anymore/

- 3 characteristics predators look for

5.27 Patterns of manipulation and control

5.28 Common pitfalls of our species/

- Should our species "master" life on Earth before trying to conquer another planet?

5.29 Does our species have what it takes to overcome and fix our chronic problems?

## **Chapter 6: The Young of Our Species** – *page 224*

6.1 Life was good as a kid, what happened?

6.2 Happy kids becoming unhappy adults

- Humans behaving as animals

6.3 What if we ask "What if"?

6.4 Three scenarios of balanced, secure environments

6.5 Removing the weeds

- Learning about inequality from a dog

6.6 Failed Human Rights

- Children and their Rights

6.7 The turning point for kids

- Comparing different types of neighborhoods?

6.8 Unbalanced now... unhealthy later? Balanced now... healthy later?

6.9 Restricting our kids using Human-made life traps

6.10 The adults responsible for the development of our species/

- The responsibility of the adults in every generation/

- Final Thoughts and Techniques for becoming a highly successful Human Being

### *Introduction/Purpose of this Book:*

It all started in the year 2010...

It finally happened. I had enough... Something was wrong. I couldn't do this anymore. I could not keep going down the same exact path that I have always gone down because the ending was always the same. It happened again. Another failed relationship. What is happening? Why do I keep ending up in the same place? Something is just not right. It can't be something I'm doing wrong...right? But what if it is me.

For the first time, I decided to just stop and think about my last few relationships. Was I missing something? Were there patterns to these failures? I started thinking back to what all my exes said about me during our time together. It hit me hard...

They all said basically the same thing about me when I was with them. However, I never heard them when I was with them, but it was clear in my head now. The reason I kept ending up in the same place is because of me, not them.

This was the first time I turned the eye-of-blame to myself. It really wasn't fun...at all. But within that hurt and shame that I felt, something new inside of me opened up. It opened up new questions about who I was and where I was going.

I then asked myself, "If I was so closed and wrong about this, what else was I wrong about?" I had to find out. What if the way I looked at my life and the world around me was just like this...wrong?

So began my adventure of figuring out how my life would be if I looked at things differently. What if I made different choices than the ones I have always made? What would my life become? What would I become? I had to find out. I was curious...

What would I become if I faced challenges in my life instead of running away from them? What would I become if I faced my fears? What would I become if I made choices about my life that were different from the people around me? I had to find out... I was curious...

*Who am I...?*

I am quite average. Average height, average weight, average looks, average intelligence...just average.

What should the reader know about the author? Should the reader know anything about the author? As I started writing this book, I, like most writers, included an "About the Author" section. While writing my background and experiences section, I suddenly stopped. I then asked myself, "What's the point?" "What's the point of the reader knowing the background of the writer?" I repeated to myself. I immediately stopped writing about myself after only two paragraphs. It felt uncomfortable. It didn't feel right.

I then asked myself, "Will the reader get more out of reading a book like this, or any book for that matter, by knowing the writer's background?" Or maybe it's the exact opposite. Maybe the reader will get more out of a book like this, or most books, if they knew less about the person writing it.

So I trashed my "About the Author" section. Why is it so important that we need to know who writes, publishes, or researches something anyway? Does the information presented to us change our opinion of that information if we know the background of the writer?

Yeah, of course it does, because we are Human. Most of us, to varying degrees, pre-judge or judge the information we gather based on the source it comes from. Of course, it can help if you know the source's background, as long as we don't allow it to alter our view of the information being presented. Hence the problem.

As Humans, many of us are filtering information as we receive it based on where that information is coming from. This obviously makes for a less intelligent brain. All received information can be used to build a smarter brain and a stronger mind, yet it doesn't matter where it comes from.

### For example:

You are asked to give your opinion on two legal documents. You are asked to read the two documents (both documents are written about the same concepts within the same context). You are told that document #1 was prepared by an Attorney (the boss) and document #2 was prepared by a Paralegal (the employee). You were told in a very casual manner who prepared each document. "Document #1 was prepared by our Attorney Micheal and document #2 was prepared for by our Paralegal John".

Those seemingly unassuming titles of Attorney and Paralegal can alter the reader's opinion before even reading it. Most likely, and more times than not, most readers will naturally have trouble separating from their pre-established biases. Most readers, me included, will read these documents with the preconceived notion that the Attorney's document will be better written and more correct than the Paralegal's.

"It has to be right. The Attorney had more schooling, has more experience. It's only natural that their document would have better and more accurate information than the Paralegal's, right?"

These are the words that lead to a certain group of thoughts in my mind. Wrong! Very wrong assumption for me to make. Even if my assumption is right about the Attorney being more educated and experienced than the Paralegal, it's what's happening in our brain that's the issue. If we have any preconceived notion that the Paralegal is any kind of less-than compared to the attorney, our mind and our brain will automatically concentrate less on document #2 and think less of it. We may even seemingly pick out more errors in the second document. Not good. By downplaying the importance of the second document that we perceive to be less than, we are missing out on the information being presented. The information being presented is much more important than the background of the person presenting it. Again, an intelligent brain can decipher good and bad information, no matter where it is coming from. An unintelligent brain is more prone to take in information from sources it is comfortable with. It's more comforting to take in the information from the Attorney than the Paralegal, although it is not necessarily right.

I started thinking long and deep one day about who and where I learned the most influential and most useful information that has benefited me the most in my own life.

It didn't take too long to figure out that the most beneficial lessons I learned in my life did not come from most adults. I started to realize that the advice I received from so many adults throughout my life was pretty much leading me nowhere. Where I would get the most beneficial lessons to life's most basic, fundamental questions and answers continually came from my observations of kids and animals... Yep, kids and animals.

To avoid the same pitfalls that I was continually making, I needed something different. I needed a new view of how the most basic, fundamental aspects of living on Earth worked on the most simplistic levels. The words and actions that I have heard and seen around me and within me up to this point in my life were just not working.

What am I missing? Why are some of us content with our lives and surroundings no matter how bad it gets, while others (like me) are content and happy only when things go their (my) way? Very Frustrating... I needed something more...

*But why kids and animals?*

They don't have a personal agenda. They don't have an angle to their actions or within their words. They don't have biases...they react. They react to the environment immediately around them. No words, no angle, no self-imposed rules and restrictions, no personal beliefs, no hate, no prejudgment to distort their actions.

This is where we can learn the tiniest details of life that exist between living things. The wordless interactions between living, breathing creatures. A child or animal will reveal how they feel about their surroundings in any number of ways. Look closely...very closely. Look for the subtleties between them; it's in their posture, the direction their eyes are gazing, their breathing, their posture, their demeanor. But these subtle non-verbal physical reactions can and will surely be missed if one chooses to speak and not think rather than observe and learn... Or if we choose to ignore the signals around them.

Much of my overall understanding of how life is supposed to work on Earth has come from countless hours of observations of kids and animals. None of these kids or animals had any degrees or much life experience.

For this reason, I will not describe who I am or what my background is. It really doesn't matter. Not for this book and not for this information. Some books and some information may be beneficial to the reader knowing about the author, but not all.

I reached a point in my life where I was ready to find out what was wrong with me. To stop blaming others for my problems. I was tired of being less-than in my life. I was tired of being looked down upon. I was tired of the same ol' life I was living. I was tired of my life being controlled by ignorant, selfish adults.

As a kid, I always felt and believed there was more. I felt and believed I was more. But as life wore on, it and I became less. Why? This couldn't be happening to my life. My life was supposed to be everything I dreamed it would be as a kid. It wasn't.

*But where do I start? I was so lost.*

Radically changing my old and only thinking patterns I knew from birth was scaring the shit out of me.

Not only did I not know where to start, I wasn't even sure if I was made up of the stuff that I needed to change...but I had to find out. I had to find out if I, someone so average, could find some peace within, some kind of sustainable confidence, some kind of hidden skills that would allow me to become independently free. Free from the personal prison I and the world around me continually created within me.

As I get older, problems seem to keep creeping up. My ability to cope with all of life's obstacles is fading. My mind is getting worse and weaker. My anger is growing. Life was never supposed to be like this. What's happening?

I began to question everything, way more than I ever did before. I was becoming miserable and did not want to continue my life this way anymore.

However, I have a trait that I have grown to admire. It is the trait that gets me out of the messes I create in my own head: I don't quit. I don't care how miserable my life is getting, I do not quit. I will not quit. I know life can be better than this, I know I can be better than this...

*But again, where do I start?*

I started thinking about my childhood a lot. What kind of kid was I before I was influenced by my environment? Influenced by society? Influenced by the adults around me?

I needed to find out what truly makes me content. I needed to figure out what kind of person I was supposed to be or could be. What gifts I may have that I didn't know about. What would the human brain—my brain—be capable of if I figured out a way to get my self-destructive mind out of its own way? Even if I never figure out the answers to these questions, not trying was not an option. I was scared of everything, especially failure. But I was tired of being scared and living with so much fear.

So, I started blending my young, past self with my older, future self (who I wanted to become); combining where I came from with where I was going.

I used to never set goals. I hated even thinking about setting goals... However, if I wanted change, I needed to do things differently. Not drastically different, just different.

So, I set a few basic goals for what I may want my life to become. Some were monthly goals, some were yearly goals, some were 5-year goals, some were 10-year goals, some were "until I die" goals. The goals each of us set for our own life are and will be unique to us depending on what we want our life to be about. Here are mine...

- Alive and still active well into old age.
- Build a more intelligent, problem-solving brain.
- Build a more creative brain.
- Build sustainable real, inner confidence.
- Master the skill of learning.
- Master one or more skills every decade of my life.
- Maintain my overall health by understanding my body and its rela-

tionship with food and exercise.

- Learn multiple musical instruments or any of the creative arts (drawing, painting, acting, etc.)
- Learn multiple foreign languages.
- Continue to find ways to enjoy every aspect of my daily life.
- Develop a sustainable self-made income (Part-time or Full-time).
- Maintain healthy relationships.
- Teach myself how to become less dependent on others.

Someone once told me to dream big. Well, there you go, I'm dreaming big. Who cares if they are not possible to achieve. I think the ride should be fun trying to figure all of this out. What's the rush anyway? I have the rest of my life to figure out me.

*Do you know what that list just gave me? It gave me purpose. It gave me purpose for the rest of my life. It also gave me a lifelong adventure...*

Many people throughout the history of mankind have mastered all of these and many more, all while maintaining a highly productive social life. There have been many Humans before us, during us, and will be after us that are mastering all areas of their life while maintaining their social life. Are they somehow greater than the rest of us? Are they genetically superior to us? There have been people throughout time who have mastered their own health, happiness, finances, emotions, relationships, intelligence, creativity, and their internal freedom along with their social life.

Why them? Why not us? Why can't our true selves be like that? Or can we?

Together we will work through these lofty goals. If others can do it, why can't we? And if we can't achieve what we set out to do, it's cool, at least we get to see what comes out of us and our brains. <u>You</u>, the reader, have a high degree of intelligence within your brain and a depth of mind that only <u>You</u> can dig out. It would seem like a waste (of our life) if we did not get out of our own way and allow our body, brain, and mind to reach its full potential. Our individual potential for intelligence, patience, emotional stability, and life-lasting internal peace is higher and more attainable than you or I could ever imagine.

*The direction of this Book...*

    As I started my lifelong personal journey, I only originally wanted to work on myself and push only myself to higher levels of life. It was overwhelming just to work on myself, much less help others. But as time went on, I started thinking that maybe I should learn how to not only become an independently-free person for myself but to be able to teach it to someone else if they wanted, especially kids.

    I definitely did not start out wanting to write a book. That was never my intention. I am not a writer, never have been. However, I learned as I would have to teach it to someone later. So, the first three chapters of the book are about me and my struggle getting myself to a higher level of living. **<u>Chapter 1</u>** is about how I changed my perspective on life. **<u>Chapter 2</u>** is about how my Human mind and my Human brain interact with one another. **<u>Chapter 3</u>** goes into great detail on how I slowly but surely changed my toxic mind into a productive mind along with a more intelligent, problem-solving brain. **<u>Chapter 4</u>** is about how we can find the time in our hectic everyday life to find ourselves and our many, many hidden gifts.

    As I studied myself intensely along with kids and animals over several years, something else started invading my thought process. I thought if I had these mind and brain challenges (problems), wouldn't most of us have them, since you know...we are all the same species? All of us Humans are 99.98% genetically the same.

**Chapter 5** is about our species. As I learned about me, kids, and animals, I learned about our species. The good and the not-so-good. Chapter five became an eye-opening, intense, sometimes very dark look at us as a species...from where we came from to where we are going.

*As I saw the life-inhibiting faults that I possessed and became more and more disgusted by them, I wondered if we all shared those. After I ripped open and exposed my many faults, I then eventually expanded to expose the faults in the city I was living in, then the state, then the country, then more countries, then eventually our entire species.*

I wrote each chapter as a stand-alone chapter. Meaning, you don't have to read the book in order. However, the first four chapters do go together and are more about finding ourselves and finding the time to find ourselves. Chapter five and Chapter six are more about our species than the individual.

**Chapter 6** ends the book taking a look at our species in its most important role... The role Human adults play as parents, role models, and teachers to our young. We will look deep into our species...the good and the not-so-good things we are doing to our kids.

This adventure I'm on within myself, although still highly active, has been incredible through its first decade. My mind and my brain have been to places I once thought were unreachable. And to me, this is only the beginning. I cannot wait to see what else I uncover in our magnificent Human brain.

_Disclaimer:_

_There is no such "one thing" that will help every single Human, no matter what we are talking about. As similar as we all are (all ~8 billion of us), we are varied in the way we perceive our surroundings, and to think a "one-size fits all" is our solution will only hold us back from becoming a strong, adaptable, independent, free person. To have variety (diversity) is to have freedom._

# Chapter 1

# Perceptive Perspective

{1.1} To understand my place in the Universe and to offer a new perspective on one's place in this world, I tried picturing myself picking up a handful of sand at the beach. I pretended each grain of sand in my hand represented a star, a planet, or a moon. Now think of all the grains of sand on this planet... All the beaches of the world (in and out of the water), all the deserts, and all the other sand I can't think of. If all those grains of sand represent planetary bodies, then we, as Humans, would be dust upon dust on a single grain of sand. Dust upon dust? A Human (dust) on a mountain (dust) on a single grain of sand (planet Earth).

Okay, so that isn't the coziest thought to have. Are we really that small and insignificant? Physically small, yes. Insignificantly small, hell no. We have to be one of the most important species of all time. We are the only current species on this planet that understands our place in the Universe. This is powerful information we have. But unfortunately, most of our species choose not to use our unique ability to make positive differences in our own lives, much less on a larger scale.

But before I can even start to worry about world problems and our species' problems, I should focus on my own issues first.

I can't remember where I heard this, but it messed with my mind for a while. It just made no sense.

**The answers to all of my problems are all around me.**

Could this be true? If so, then most of us should be really close to figuring out what's causing our problems? It sure doesn't seem that way though. Surely not for me. I don't feel close at all to solving my problems. Feels like I'm getting further away from solving my issues.

**The answers to all of my problems are all around me.**

*Where?* I can't see them. I want to see them but I can't! This kind of advice must be wrong, right?

Wrong? No. This is actually pretty good advice. I just can't see what I am not looking at. But if we are looking at ourselves and still can't find it, it's okay, it takes time. Most importantly, we are looking at ourselves for our issues in our life, not at others. I personally had a very hard time looking at myself and my own faults and the problems I caused. My continual blaming of others for my problems was hiding the answers to my problems. The answers to my problems are all around me because they are me.

*I am my biggest problem...*

It would be an understatement to say it was rough to realize this about myself. I am my problem. That just plain sucks. I would much rather blame others for my problems. Of course, that seems to put me back in the same spot I always end up; not content with my life...miserable.

These kinds of thoughts hurt and cut deep. I wasn't perfect... My opinion wasn't always right... Some people don't like me... I would then obsess about how pitiful my life was... I would begin to loathe in self-pity.

{1.2} So I identified a problem. When a few things in my life go bad, I start to withdraw and hate. I didn't want to help others like I normally do. I had less patience. I lied more. I complained more. I came up with more excuses...

When a few things went well, my attitude changed...for the better, of course. I could be the best me at any time when things were going my way but when things did not go the way I wanted, all of a sudden life started to suck all over again. Um...what?

I started getting mad at myself. Really mad. I'm a coward. I'm great when life is good, and I suck when life is challenging. Something is off. I'm off.

*...I'm spiraling down. My mind is not good. What do I do? I'm scared...*

Not a good place to be. But because of recurring scenarios like this, I was finally inclined to do something different. When my thoughts spiraled down, I needed a quick mind change. I started to force myself to have honest conversations about myself, with myself. Why force? It fitted my personality better than not forcing. I needed to make myself uncomfortable. Change is uncomfortable. Growth can be uncomfortable.

**{1.3}** *Sample conversation I have with myself in my head.*

*(Me)* in the conversation is my mind and *(Myself)* is my brain. For the most part, my mind is the neurotic, paranoid, unrealistic worrier, problem-creator while my brain, when allowed to, is the common sense, realistic problem solver.

*Me (my mind):* Do you think I can actually be happy in this crazy world?

*Myself (my brain):* Um...yes.

*Me:* Have you seen the news? Have you been in public? Getting pretty crazy. And I over-analyze and get overly concerned about all of this?

*Myself:* Yes I have seen it. You and I are one and the same. However, when allowed to, I choose to see things differently than you from time to time.

*Me (my mind):* How the hell are you seeing what I'm seeing differently than me?

*Myself (my brain):* Do you remember what I told you?

*Me:* About what? I don't pay attention to much of what you say.

*Myself:* I know and that's why you are where you have always been.

*Me:* And where is that?

*Myself:* Somewhere between judgmental, negative, and self-righteousness.

*Me:* Sounds familiar.

*Myself:* It should. It's where you go when life goes a little astray. Remember, your personality has a very good, strong-minded side. However, when not balanced, the not-so-good, weak-minded side comes out.

*Me:* Well, how do I do more of the good and less of the bad?

*Myself:* Good question. I'm glad we are finally having this conversation. Much of our long term happiness comes from having hope or a way out. Remember, all living things will always strive to be free. One way to be mentally "free" is to have hope.

*Me:* Hope? Really? What the hell does hope have to do with me dealing with everyday *bullshit?* I need something better than hope to help me.

*Myself:* Well if you had some patience and thought things through and oh...I don't know...be a little more open-minded, you would be able to see things differently.

*Me:* Still not seeing the stupid "Hope" connection.

*Myself:* Ok.

*Myself:* Broaden your view and change your perspective. "All of your answers to all of your problems are all around you". We will start slowly by slowing down, being more observant of our surroundings, developing some patience, and never stop learning.

*Me:* This is deep. I would rather think about anything else but this. This hurts, it's frustrating and lame and I don't like it.

*Myself:* This is why we don't change. This is why our life will always be the way it is.

*Me:* Screw that. I want something different. I just don't like working on things deep within me that hurts and feels uncomfortable.

*Myself:* Yeah, and that's where the answers to our problems will be found. Behind that pain, lameness, and discomfort.

*Me:* Not cool at all.

*Me:* Still not getting hope though.

*Myself:* Whenever you are stuck in a tough spot in life, it's always good to have a go-to "tool" that you can use to get you "out". If a plumber is fixing a toilet and their first tool isn't doing the job, they go to the next tool. This second plumbing tool works a little better than the first and gets the job a little further along but eventually doesn't finish the job as well. They go to a third tool. There is no third tool. The plumber relied too heavily on the first two tools while disregarding the importance of having a wide selection of tools. The job will now take much longer and take more money to complete. Frustration sets in. If they had a few more tools or *options* to go to, the latter part of the scenario probably wouldn't have happened.

*Me:* You and your analogies. What does that have to do with hope?

*Myself:* That "go-to tool" in life is what your brain has, hopefully, to give you several options to get out of life's sticky situations. Everyone will go through the highs and lows of life. It's how each individual person handles and perceives each situation that separates the successful and content Humans from the not-so successful and not-so-content Humans. Don't you remember the last 18 months? The last 18 months have been the most challenging of our life and look at how well we did through it all. We changed, the world around us didn't; it actually got worse while we got better. We should be very proud of that. It was not easy.

*Me:* I am.

*Myself:* Good.

*Myself:* So to have more "tools" means that we have given our brain or mind lots of options to get out of any uncomfortable situation we may encounter in life. That gives us hope for any of those uncomfortable, challenging situations we will surely encounter. Having hope that was created by you gives you Inner Confidence. A lot of it. And that Inner Confidence we created for ourselves allows us to become not only us, but the better, freer version of us. And that is the version I want to be every day because it's awesome and life becomes so much more fulfilling when we have personal freedom and self-built hope.

*Me:* Sounds good to me!

{1.4} Why am I built this way? Why does my mind tend to bring me misery? Is my mind interpreting my surroundings correctly? If my mind works like this, others must work like this as well, right

Absolutely. There is usually somebody out there that processes information much like us. Do they handle it like I would, or do they handle it differently? How different are we really from each other?

Let's start at the species level. There are approximately eight billion of us individuals that make up our species. At the current reproductive rate, we will double that number in the next 50 years. Eight billion is a lot before doubling. But as different as we seem over the entirety of our species, we are vastly more similar than different. On a genetic level, we are 99.99% the same. All eight billion of us. For the most part and for most of us; our bodies, minds and brains operate similarly to one another on a biochemical (chemical interactions deep within our cells), biological (life giving processes), physiological (how our body works), and psychological (our brain and mind connection) level.

{1.5} Using an intelligence example, the top 5% of our species (a 10 on a scale from 0-10) would represent the genetically rare, highly, out-of-the ordinary smart person. This type of person is born smart, not made intelligent through their environment. The same goes for the bottom 5% (a 0 (zero) on a scale of 1-10). These individuals would have true congenital (born with) learning disabilities, not caused by their environment.

The other 90% is the rest of us. It doesn't matter if you are born as a genetic 1 or 9 (on a scale from 0-10) or anything in between, you are most likely not locked into that number. Meaning, the other 90% of our species, the 1's through 9's can be influenced (able to move up and down the scale) by their environment, good or bad, up or down. This pattern virtually holds true for everything we talk about in this book and well, life too *(when dealing with genetic versus environmental influences over our life)*. We have much more control over our intelligence, our patience, our long-term vision, our health, our purpose, our life, than we were taught. We can alter and enhance our own environment that is independent of our genetics.

It also means that 90% of us are extremely similar in more ways than one.

Supposedly there are 16 personality types, so we'll use that number as a reference point. There are approximately eight billion of us on this planet. 8,000,000,000/16= 500,000,000. That means half a billion people on this planet have a very similar core personality like you, regardless of their ethnic origin (no matter where they are from).

{1.6} For most of us, the 1 through 9s, the type and amount of information our brains receive has an enormous influence over how our brains develop. The human brain, therefore the human, is more powerful when highly diversified.

You decide: Which brain will become more of a powerful, intelligent problem solver over time?

### Brain A

1 - Receives continual information that is similar in content.

2 - Closed to receiving new information.

3 - Judges before learning.

4 - Learns one or two skills in a lifetime.

5 - Thinks it knows everything.

6 - Discounts information because "it doesn't apply to me."

*Or...*

## <u>Brain B</u>

1 - Receives information of diversified content.

2 - Open to receiving new information.

3 - Learns before judging.

4 - Continuously learns new skills throughout life.

5 - Knows it does not know everything.

6 - Adds information because "it may apply to me later."

My mind's ability to separate and *not* connect what happens in my life to anything else around me is quite fascinating.

For the longest time I couldn't figure out that having a high diversity of thoughts and experiences actually makes my life easier. Half a billion people on this planet are mostly like me (like you), regardless of state, country, continent, or ethnicity. Diversity must be one of the keys to having a successful life.

Ever wonder how you and your personality would fair living in another country under different living conditions? Think you would do okay?

*Those kinds of thoughts would scare me. "No way could I make it in another country with different living conditions," I would think to myself. I was too scared to leave the town, much less the country. I had to face the truth of what I was becoming. I was not developing an adaptable personality at all. I was a coward. I was fearful of change. I was fearful of failure. I was fearful of what people thought of me... I no longer wanted to be this way.*

Speaking of a different place, what about a different time period? A lot of people with my personality type have come and gone over the last few thousand years, millions and millions of them actually. How would my personality hold up if I lived 3000 years ago or 300 years ago? What about my personality in 300 years or 3000 years into the future?

I get caught up in the idea trap that the current generation of Humans are better than our predecessors. Why? Is it because we have more and better technology? It doesn't add up. The human brain has been around much longer than any technology. It really doesn't matter how much better technology gets, our human brains, our human minds, have not changed much in the last few thousand years. It can be counter-productive to our own intelligence to separate the worthiness of Humans by the generations that they lived in. It's counterproductive because our brains will "tune out" and choose not to receive and learn from any information about earlier generations if we allow our minds to *discount* it. Bad idea. An intelligent brain rarely "tunes out" or disregards information. Allowing myself to envision me and my personality and how I would live in a different time period gives my brain more information to make more connections, which will eventually allow for a more intelligent brain.

{**1.7**} A balanced, diverse perspective is essential to developing a brain and mind with high intelligence.

*Me (my mind):* Why? Couldn't I max out my intelligence by becoming really good at one or two things throughout my life?
*Myself (my brain):* Let's think about this. Are you asking this?

*Hypothetical situation: A man becomes a banker after he graduates from college at age 24. He works hard and moves up the ranks throughout his 40 years as a banker. He becomes a top banker in his region. He is regarded as a great banker, one of the best. Wealthy. Intelligent. Well-liked. Well-respected...*

*Wealthy? Yeah. Well-liked? Sure. Well-respected? Maybe. Intelligent? To whom? To whom is this person intelligent? Is he regarded as intelligent by all or by his closest circle of friends?*

<u>Me</u>: Um...where are you going with this?

<u>Myself</u>: First off, intelligence is relative to what you think you think intelligence is. This banker may seem intelligent from the perspective of himself or from the perspective of others in his circle, but how intelligent could you realistically be if you only studied one or two trades with one or two types of people with similar mentalities your entire adult life?

<u>Me</u>: Oh...okay, I'm getting it now

<u>Myself</u>: Well, you can become very intelligent depending on many other factors outside of your career. If you have many varied hobbies to go along with your banking career, then yes, you can begin to max out your own personal intelligence.

<u>Me</u>: What about the banker who only cares about banking and doesn't give two shits about wasting time on hobbies?

<u>Myself</u>: Do you think it is possible for that type of person to max out his/her intellectual genetic potential? It would be highly unlikely. How could it? Again, we decide for ourselves:

## **<u>Banker Brain A</u>**

- Graduated top of their class.

- Has a family pedigree of bankers, many generations.

- Studies only banking and finance related activities.

**Or...**

## Banker Brain B

- Graduated in the top half of their class.

- 1st generation banker.

- Studies banking and many other non-financial activities.

...

## Brain A

1- Receives information using only 1 or 2 of our 5 senses.

2- Receives information with no intent to make connections to anything received previously received.

**Or...**

## Brain B

1- Receives information using 4-5 of our 5 senses.

2- Allows currently received information to make connections to previously received information while using 4-5 senses.

*Myself:* Just because I may think I am smart and my first thoughts "have never felt more right," that doesn't automatically make me a smart person.

*Me:* I don't know about that. Lots of people have told me to go with the first thing that comes to mind and act fast on it. "What are you waiting for!!" they scream in my head. Those first thoughts that pop in my head have to be right. Why would I think those exact thoughts first? It must mean it's important, right?

*Myself:* No, not necessarily. It's how you use your brain that allows you to max out our intellectual potential. Even when allowing our brain to receive information using all of our senses, it is still not enough. Allowing our brain to make connections with new, incoming information with as much past information as we can is critical for development. \*\*\*

Remember, for us to develop into a highly adaptable Human, we need high variation in life. So, it seems to make sense for us to use the past, the present, and future information as much as we can. To not think about and include all three with, at the very least, our major life decisions, would hide so much valuable information from us. To hide information from ourselves is damaging to ourselves.

{1.8} Also, the more we do this, the more we will work on making this a repeated habit. A good habit. A better, stronger nervous system (brain, spinal cord) along with more connections will follow. The more connections we make with present and past information, the stronger electrical (neural) connections are built within us, making us stronger. And because we made it important, the brain will also make it important, which will trigger the start of the building up of a massive network of strong neural connections that makes us highly adaptable. **Adaptable Humans are successful Humans.**

{1.9} For most of my life, I was terrible with directions. I would get lost everywhere. It was so bad at one point that I even got lost in a parking lot. Yep, that's kind of pathetic. I felt really dumb. How could I get lost in a parking lot? I must be stupid, right?

Almost immediately, I started making excuses as to why I am bad with directions. It's quite amusing the excuses the human mind can come up with when you are the one making the mistakes. I actually started telling others that I may have some bad genetics when it comes to figuring out directions. Wow! What an excuse! *Genetics? Really?* Bad genetics made me bad at directions? It actually made some sense.

My parents and other relatives were also bad at directions, so it must be a genetic thing...right?

I was so convincing to myself and to others that I started believing it. It became part of me. And guess what my brain did (automatically) as soon as I blamed it on genetics? It began to filter. It began to filter information about directions. This kind of filter was the type with the tiniest of holes. Those tiniest of holes didn't let much pass. From that point on in my life, my brain would waste little to no time and little to no energy when it came to anything involving directions. If the mind told itself it was genetics and discounted it for any reason, the brain would expend very little energy in regards to "learning" when anything about directions came up. In other words, if our mind makes it unimportant, then our brain will make it unimportant, barely using our senses to gather more information. "How could I get better at directions if it's a genetic deficiency?" I would whisper to myself in my head. So just like that, in a matter of two seconds, I put up roadblocks in my brain when it came to learning about getting better at directions. Why would my brain devote any time or energy to smelling, seeing, listening, touching, or tasting anything about getting better at directions if I told myself it was a genetic defect, even without me trying to test to show if my assumption was wrong or not?

*Something was wrong all right...*
*... My illogical, unrealistic thinking.*

My genetic excuse may possibly be true, but without me trying to see if it is not, it didn't really make much sense either.

For most of my life I believed, with everything I had, that my problems with directions and getting lost was a genetic problem that has been passed down. Someone even told me that all I need to do is observe more and pay attention to details when I enter someplace. So my response to that was, "Yeah, I'm sure that would help some but I got unlucky with the direction gene that I inherited. So, I can't and won't be able to get better even if I keep trying."

...ugh...

...that word can't. What a terrible word.

As I go through life directionless, I continue to get lost over and over. Until one day I saw something. I was intensely observing something unfold before me that made me realize that my genetic excuse wasn't holding up.

I was watching a six-year-old walking deep into an agricultural crop field. The field wasn't planted at the time but all the rows were made. I was looking over this several hundred acre field of dirt rows. Every row looked nearly identical. The six-year-old walked over 100 yards (300 feet) into the field while criss-crossing several rows. She found a particular stick she liked.

"It looks like a snake!" she screamed. "Come see it!"

I yelled back, "Okay, but give me a few minutes." I was in the middle of helping a three-year-old walk through the rough terrain.

She then walked back to where she started. She told her friend to come check out the cool stick she found deep in the fields. I was watching with high interest. I knew I wouldn't be able to find it and I sure didn't think a six-year-old could find her way back to a small, very specific area in a featureless field.

*This is much harder than my parking lot,* I was thinking as I was following her. I couldn't keep my eyes from what happened next...

The field was very dry so tracks were not helping. As she walked back and forth, over and over again, her frustration level was growing. She could not find the stick, but she would not give up. She did something next that changed something in me.

She went to the beginning and started again. This time, walking much slower but much more aware and observant of her surroundings. She was recalling the details from her first walk out into the field.

As she looked back at us, she said, "Yeah, I remember this spot from the first time."

Every few steps she would take, she would stop and scan her surroundings, looking around her while also looking back to where she started.

She was, without thinking about it, using spatial information she gathered during the first walk to help her narrow down the area where the stick might have been. Even after all of this, I was still somewhat doubtful of her finding it.

She then screamed, "I found it! Come see!"

I couldn't believe it. She found it...and something changed in me in an instant. Was I wrong? Was my genetics excuse wrong? Were all my excuses I've told myself over and over my entire life wrong as well?

*{1.10}* I had to put what I saw into action. Was she just genetically good at figuring out directions? Did she learn this from somebody? Was she taught directly, or did she observe someone doing this?

How would I find something like this out?

Well, I just asked her. I said to her, "You're pretty good at figuring out your surroundings. How did you learn how to do that?"

**{Notice how I did not ask her "who" or "where" she learned it. The more open-ended word "how" allows for openness and for her <u>Not</u> to guide her response in a certain direction to my question. Saying "who" to a child may accidentally guide the child's direction into an answer that's not completely accurate.**

**It's all in the subtleties of life. They can slowly tear you down or slowly build you up.}**

She answered, "My Dad showed me how to be observant and pay attention to my surroundings when I go to a new place."

So, I told her Dad what she said and what she did in the field. He became ecstatic and overjoyed. He then went into more detail of what and how he taught her. As he was explaining how he taught her I was thinking of her in the field. As he explained it, I could see her acting out his words in that field. It was an incredible parenting moment.

*{1.11}* I still needed to figure out if I was genetically impaired when it came to directions. Could I get better at directions at my age? At any age? Or was it my ability to disregard the useful information around me and not genetics? I had to find out.

"It just can't be. I can't be this damn pathetic at directions, right? It must be something else," I would tell myself.

Well, there aren't many ways to find out if it's me, or my genetics, or some other excuse I haven't come up with yet. I knew what I had to do. I had to force myself to try to learn how to get better at navigating my surroundings without getting lost.

I started small and familiar with my neighborhood. I looked at my neighborhood differently for the first time after living there for several decades. I began to notice new things every day that I never noticed before. These are the same places I have passed my entire existence. I drove in small circles around my neighborhood trying to learn; which streets run North and South? Which direction is North and South when standing in front of my house? Where does the sun rise and set in relation to my house, my neighborhood? Any tall or recognizable features? Etc...

It felt weird doing this and it also made me feel really dumb. I didn't know any of this about my house or my neighborhood. And I'm also bad at figuring all this out. But if a kid could do it, I could, I thought. I kept pushing. I had to see. I had to see what would happen...

I kept doing this over and over throughout the next several months. I was quite amazed how much I was improving at not getting lost by just slowing down and paying more attention to the details around me. I had to really test it though. Not in the streets, but in the deep woods. And not with daylight either, at night.

Could I, a self-diagnosed genetically impaired navigator, find my way through a dark forest with only a flashlight? No map of any kind, no GPS, no trail markers, just me and a flashlight...

Not only did I find my way, I found my way in and out a ½ mile back into those deep, dark woods.

That walk in and out of the woods changed me. I worked on something that I was always bad at. I even blamed genetics. Never did I blame it on myself. "I just couldn't be the problem," I would always tell myself.

That walk changed my perspective on the validity of my excuses. I've used excuses for lots of things throughout my life. And I've also used the, "Oh, it must be genetics, or it must be this or it must be that, it can't be something I'm doing wrong."

If I was wrong about this, could I be wrong about my other excuses? I had to find out.

*{1.12}* Let's end this chapter by going back to the beginning of this chapter. We started this journey through this chapter with this sentiment: The answers to my problems are all around me. Continually thinking I was never the problem in my life while continually making excuses about anything and everything, never really got me anywhere.

When I decided to turn my desire of judging others onto myself, things changed. I figured I wasn't any better than anyone else. In fact, when I started judging my life like I would judge others, I started to see I was less than the people I was judging. "What makes me better than anyone else?" I would begin to ask myself...

"Absolutely nothing!!"

As much as I loathed the idea of turning my vicious criticism onto myself, I knew I had to. I had to do something different. I was going down a dangerous road. A road I did not want to go down; the selfish, the self-absorbed, the close-minded, the my-needs-first road. This road was getting more and more bumpy, and I wanted to get off but I had no clue how or where to start. I was starting to show my age physically and emotionally.

What happened to my life? I was happy as a kid. (I, gratefully, had, for the most part, a happy childhood). Why was I becoming more and more unhappy the older I got?

{1.13} I was often told by numerous adults while growing up, "Stay a kid, being an adult isn't as great as it seems".

Why? Why are so many adults unhappy? Is it just an age thing? Not likely. I have met happy, content, successful, productive adults of all ages.

So, where or what is the missing link? Why can some of us achieve this while others struggle with finding it?

To solve a problem like this, or any problem really, it helped me to look at it from as many different angles and perspectives as I could.

_Reminder to Me and Myself:_ Something that is hidden can lead to fear. "Under the bed" is scary because you can't see what's there. Your mind will then make up something that's suddenly lurking in those *deep, dark corners underneath your bed. If you remove everything from underneath your bed and light up those dark corners (some parents raise their kids beds and puts night lights underneath the beds to reduce the possibility of their child's mind making up something that's underneath the bed), you highly reduce the chance that your mind will develop a fear of the space under which you sleep.*

### **It's hard to fear something after you expose it as nothing!!**

I used to be so clueless as to how houses were built. What was behind the wall was just as scary as what was at the bottom of a deep lake. So, fixing something in my house was out of the question. I was too scared of what might happen if I start working on something that I knew very little about. I would always call someone who could fix it. I was dependent on others to keep my own house running. Not a good feeling.

It was when I was forced to go through the wall of my house to do a major repair job that I could not afford to pay someone else to do. I finally saw the guts of my house. I finally saw how a house was built and how it runs. I finally saw how stupid I was for being scared and fearful of what was behind the wall. Once it was exposed, the fear left, and the confidence entered.

I started to force myself to do the opposite of what I wanted to do. I forced myself to look at my problems from as many levels and perspectives as I could. I figured if I could expose as many places I had in my dark-mind, my fears would start to go away. I used a microscope-type technique to "reveal" the layers of my problems. From micro to macro. From the tiniest perspectives to the largest. From the physical to the meta-physical.

*It's not the trees in the Forest. It's the fluid that flows through the veins within the leaves on the branches of those trees within that Forest.*

So, I forced myself to look at my problems from any and every level and angle I could think of. But—and this is a Big But—I made sure I started taking responsibility for my actions, especially my wrongdoings of others.

As I revealed more and more layers of perspectives, I had to keep reminding myself to take blame. I'll talk more about why this seemingly minor step was easily one of the most beneficial thoughts I've ever had.

Before I dove into the historical and biological relevance of my problems, I told myself not to forget this: "No matter what I uncover and reveal, remember that most of the problems I think I have are just that." Think = Thoughts.

Some of my problems are real and unavoidable. Some. Most, however, are just that, thoughts. Life around us, for the most part, doesn't change much. It will be a constant ride of ups and downs. No matter who you are or where you come from, life is consistently inconsistent. And the quote, "The only thing you can change is you," is quite accurate. You and I can maybe change some people in our life but the real change usually starts and ends with me and you.

As for the biological relevance of our problems, we can and should explore the possibility of a genetic basis for our problems, but we have many other angles to consider before blaming it on genetics. Learning how we live and respond to our surroundings from a species-perspective versus an individual-within-a-species reveals and opens many hidden spaces in the mind. Less hidden spaces...less fear. More openness...higher peace of mind...higher intelligence.

As for historical relevance, exploring and thinking about our place in our family tree can bring in an abundance of information. We can think about something like our birth order (first child, middle child, last child), which influences our behavior as well as our ancestors' several generations before us, in regard to how they lived and responded to their environment. As stupid as that sounds, "What could my ancestors from 100 years ago have anything to do with me and my current problems?" It's called Epigenetics. It's how our environment (everything outside of our DNA) influences (turns on or turns off) our genes. It's powerful. Our genes change often. They are heavily influenced by what you and I do and where and how you and I do it.

"But still. What does that have to do with my ancestors? You obviously can't change what they did," I would ask myself. No, we can't, but we can learn about how they lived. It can give you clues to who you are. The real you. It may offer insight to our fears. Maybe, most importantly, learning about your ancestors takes the pressure off of you being you. It's a comforting feeling to learn that there are others out there struggling with the same things we do. Anytime we have the opportunity to take pressure off of us being us, take it.

# Chapter 2

# Mind My Brain

{2.1} If someone walked up to you right now and asked you to describe the difference between the brain and the mind... What would you say? What would your description be?

I would have struggled answering that question years ago. Now, however, after thinking, digging, and learning for the last several years, my answer to that question has become a little clearer.

*Here is my attempt to separate the two:*

The brain is the physical, somewhat squishy organ that sits between our ears. The mind, however, is this somewhat non-physical cloud-like invisible structure that filters information entering and exiting the brain. It's an ever-changing filter.

What kind of filter? Well first, what's the point of a filter? Easy, to allow some things to pass through and some things not to. The Human mind is our brain filter that we control. We control the size of the holes in that filter. We control the rate of flow through that filter. We control our filters (minds). Our brains are then developed or not developed because of our filters and ultimately our control over our filters.

### *Simplify before we complicate*

{2.2} Most of the answers to most of our problems are simple yet overlooked. The brain is much like a computer but much more powerful. A computer takes in information and stores it for later use by the operator. The more information (programs/apps) that is fed into the computer, the more ability of the computer. Then connections between the programs occur. The more connections between the programs and the more communications between the programs, the more power the computer has.

*What kind of power?*

The computer, with the addition of a variety of programs and apps, will gain the ability to use past information from earlier programs to connect to information received from the new, recently installed programs/apps. Meaning, computers can use and do use past information with current information. Why would it not? More connected information makes the computer much stronger and more intelligent.

Our computer is only worth the information it has in it and what it can do with that information. Less information, less information to work with, less ability to problem solve. Guess what happens when the computer has less ability to solve problems? Problems creep up. Continually.

*If our brain is like a computer, then what would our mind be?*

Me. I control what programs are put on the computer. I have full control of the types of programs that are installed on my computer's long-term hard drives.

### Eerily similar to how our brain and mind works

The brain in your head right now is more powerful than any computer. Any person reading this possesses a brain that is more powerful than any computer. How, you ask? Easy, the Human brain built the computer. No Human brain, no computer. Your brain, my brain, our Human brains, are capable of much. However, the brain, much like its computer counterpart, is limited to using what it receives. The brain cannot fix something it knows nothing about.

And just like we are the filter of what programs are loaded onto our computer, we are also the filter of our brain. Our mind is that filter.

{2.3} The more we let unbiased information enter our brain, the stronger it gets. As it gets stronger, it builds stronger and more efficient networks of deep, dense neural connections. These well-built neural connections will be remembered for decades to come and with more connections, we have more ways to figure out our problems. As long as you have a way out, we give the Human brain hope. Having hope is damn good. Very good for our brain. Hope is a very strong brain builder. If we give our brains hope along with a wide variety of skills, there's not much it can't do.

Let's go back to the first sentence of the last paragraph. There is one word in that sentence that can have extraordinary implications in what kind of brain we are trying to build...

...*unbiased*.

This is one of the most important states of mind one can enter. To allow our mind and thoughts to step out of the way and let our brain gather information that is presented as-is—no personal angle, need, or want behind it—can be incredibly difficult for many. It was very difficult for me. I believe it's a major flaw of the Human mind. Our first thoughts and impressions tend to be filtered in a selfish way. This is not a good thing as it will present you and I with continual challenges. But if we are aware of it and the long-term damage it can do, the easier we can steer away from it.

If I want to build a stronger, healthier, more intellectual, problem-solving brain, why the hell would I allow my distorted, biased, selfish perceptions to be the filter of incoming information?

I have been extremely close-minded for most of my life. To open my mind up to new unfiltered information was painful to say the least, but I was determined to change. I had to push through the lows. And some of those lows were very low. I needed change and I needed it badly. I needed to and had to radically change the way I viewed the world around me. It was time. NO more excuses.

*So, I tried it... Yep, as promised, it sucked.*

To allow unrestricted information to enter my brain without my initial opinion, without my wants, without my needs, was deeply challenging. We Humans have a naturally built-in mind that filters the vast majority of information coming our way. We have to, we are under constant bombardment of incoming information. Very little of this information makes its way into the deep recesses of the brain. What type of information would those recesses of the brain allow to enter that deep? I would imagine whatever information my mind would repeatedly make important.

Whichever thought I chose to think about more than the other thoughts would most likely be the thoughts allowed to go through the many filters and enter the deep recesses of the brain. Another way that our brain would allow information to enter the deep brain is if that incoming information can be harmful or helpful later in life.

{2.4} It was excruciatingly hard to view and accept ways that made no sense in my mind. I wanted to try anything but this. But I had to. I had to force myself to do something different. I had to force myself to change because I wasn't happy about how my life was turning out. It hurt. This hurt. It hurt to force change in myself. It hurt to look at things differently. It didn't feel right. I was starting to come up with as many excuses as I could to not do this. I was talking to myself and telling myself that it was okay to stay the way we are. My life isn't that bad......but that was my weak mind speaking.

*My brain and strong mind shutting down the wasteful thoughts in my weak mind:*
*"Hell no, we have to stop thinking like that. We can't always take the easy way out. We need to force change in our own selves. It's time. It's about to hurt but not all hurt is bad. Some hurt is good, as it allows for growth."*

Someone once told me that the answers to my own personal problems are right behind the hurt I keep avoiding. Could they be right? I had to find out. No matter how long it took. No matter how hard this gets. No matter how much it hurts, we push on. I needed to see for myself if that was true for me, my mind, and my brain.

"Could the answers to my problems be where my mind doesn't want to go?" I would ask myself. "Is it in the pain that lies deep down within me?"

*A Human mind that avoids the heart of the problem will most likely lead to the building of a brain that is incomplete and weaker than a brain that is accompanied by a mind that does not avoid the true reasons for their own problems.*

A strong mind, which I wish I had when I was younger, allows any and all information to enter. No biased filters. No personal agendas. No self-driven angle. A strong mind allows the brain time to evaluate the information presented.

*The more open and adaptable our mind is, the stronger and more equipped our brain will become.*

But how do we do this? Before we get into that we need to take a huge step back, widen our perspective, and take a look at what's in front of us.

{2.5} So how do we widen our perspective? Well, I started to imagine I was a mile high into the sky above us looking down. What would I be looking at? I wouldn't see me. I wouldn't see any of us as individuals. I would be able to see what we built as a species, but I would not be able to see any of us. Already, at just one mile up, we become invisible. Even looking down from the top of a really tall building, what do we look like from there? Insects. Insects scurrying in all directions; seemingly meaningless patterns of movement. A whole bunch of individuals living as one. From the top of that tall building, even us, an incredibly complex species, look nothing more than a bunch of ants on an anthill scurrying in seemingly random directions.

{2.6} This kind of thinking opened up many more questions. How similar are we? How different are we? How is it that some of us are happy and content no matter what life throws at us, while others (myself included) seem to just to go through life without really living and who constantly struggle with life's challenges?

I decided to dig and dig and keep digging until I found something. Maybe I should be looking at this from a larger perspective, from a species-level perspective. I will need to expose my brain. Expose it to any and all possibilities while removing all biases created by my mind and let my brain do its job.

*To understand how my mind works with the brain I was born with, I have to do some simplifying. I have a Human brain. You have a Human brain. We all have a Human brain. Even though our minds want to see it differently, in reality, our brains are all very similar.*

*Eight billion of us. That's a lot. However, we all are 99.99% genetically identical. Now, that 0.01% in the world of genes can serve for the noticeable and unnoticeable differences between us. But for the most part, we are all very similar. Which is important because anybody you meet throughout your time on this planet can serve as an important source of information about a Human behavior that you may be unfamiliar with. Those who are wise choose to learn from the many people they come across throughout their lives instead of avoiding those who are different.*

*So then, if we are so similar to one another, why are some of us happier than others? More successful than others? More peaceful than others?*

*Is it mostly our environment then? Is our environment more powerful than our genetics? Is the environment that surrounds us during our entire upbringing more powerful than the genes we were born with?*

{2.7} Was I like an ant who followed the paths made by many or was I like an ant who thought on my own and created my own, unique path? Not all ants followed the same paths. I, like many ants, was content with following the main flow of life. Doing what so many others around me were doing as they were doing what so many others were doing around them.

And I was also a jealous person. I was jealous of everyone and everything. I wanted what they had. I wanted their happiness. I wanted their job. I wanted their relationships. I wanted their money. I was so stupid. Why was I so jealous? I even thought about how wasteful that way of thinking was. Out of all the wasteful human emotions we go through, this one needs to be at the top of the list. Being jealous of anyone for anything is a huge waste of our time. Our mind and brain will be much better off doing anything else.

So I decided to turn my jealousy into something more productive. If I wanted to be jealous of someone, I should learn why. No more excuses. I need to find out why I keep behaving like this. Being jealous makes me feel like a less-than, yet I keep behaving this way.

For the better part of a decade I studied, observed, and acquired as much information as I could about me and about my surroundings to find that internal peace-of-mind I so badly wanted. I needed to find me. I wanted to find out what I was made of.

What do I become if I base my decisions on what I need biologically or emotionally, not on selfish material needs and wants? What do I become if I remove my self-prescribed fears and self-doubts? What am I capable of? If other Humans throughout human history achieved great things with virtually the same exact brain that you and I have in our heads right now, why can't we do it?

My core personality goals through this time became simpler and simpler the more I learned. The more I learned and explored about our species, the more I wanted this...to just be okay with me. I just wanted to be comfortable with who I was, all of my faults and all of my strengths.

*I just wanted to find peace among the chaos and to be able to find peace when I needed it.*

That was it. That was my lifelong adventure now; to find out what makes me me and how I can continually find my own peace of mind no matter what happens around me. This was undoubtedly going to be a bumpy, challenging, yet worthwhile journey.

Back to jealousy. See what can happen when we allow our mind to alter reality's perception, especially with something as dreadful as jealousy? Our intellectual brain is only as powerful as our mind will let it be. When I thought about how many hours, days, weeks, months of my life that I wasted on being jealous of someone or something while also never doing anything to correct it, it damn near shut down every bit of jealousy I ever had. It still took a little while to completely be jealous-free, but that thought process about how wasteful jealousy really was, was the turning point. My jealousy over anyone or anything quickly went away when I could see the long-term damage to myself along with the time and energy I lost. I was out.

If I could do this with jealousy, could I expose the wastefulness of other traits I possess and extinguish them as well?

This relates back to how different or similar we are to one another. Let's look at Human intelligence again or any other Human trait for the most part. Are some of us that much smarter or dumber than the rest of us? Intelligence is just like most other traits; they fall into a bell-shaped curve that is driven by the environment we create more than the genetics we possess.

The 90/10 breakdown represents 90% environmental influences (*developed in*) versus 10% genetic influences (*born with*). These percentages follow very closely to many (not all) genetic trait breakdowns within the Human population. Height, weight, skin color, and many others follow the same environmentally-induced pattern. Even most diseases follow the same pattern.

Type I Diabetes *(the one where we are insulin dependent, we don't make our own insulin so it must be injected. Insulin lowers our blood sugar naturally)*. This is the mostly genetic one. Type II Diabetes is mostly tied to our environment that we created *(you make insulin but cannot use it at all or cannot use it properly)*. Same bell curve breakdown. If you surveyed 100 diabetic patients, you would most likely find that 5-10% of them had the genetic Type I while the other 90-95% would have the environmentally induced Type II.

Same for Cancer. Ninety percent of cancers are environmentally induced and mostly created by our species. Only about 5-10% of cancers are genetically induced and have been around for hundreds of millions of years. Which means, when we change our environment, we change our chance of getting cancer, higher or lower. Most diseases that kill us today are much more human/environment-induced than genetically-induced.

So why wouldn't intelligence follow the same pattern? About 1-5% of us are genetically highly intelligent. That's 5 out of 100 people (1 out of 20). Five people out of a packed movie theater may have high genetic intelligence. They may not use it correctly, but they possess it. The same goes for the bottom 1-5% of the intelligence spectrum. Those Humans possess real, genetically-induced learning disabilities. **\*\* These percentages can and may fluctuate depending on what part of the Human species we are looking at.**

However, that means for the rest of us, the 90%, are pretty much the same in regard to genetic potential intelligence. So, if 90% of kids in a classroom have similar potential genetic intelligence, why is there such a discrepancy and separation between them?

Where or what else can it be? The 90% of the kids in the classroom who are not the genetically low 5% or the genetically high 5% must be influenced by something else, right? There aren't very many places to look. The environment surrounding these kids during their developmental years is it. For the most part, with most kids, adults, caretakers, mentors and everyone in between cultivates and molds the 90% of us. The adults are the environment. Adults make the environment, good or bad, stimulating or inhibiting.

Except for a few rare cases (0.1-5%) of people with genetic limitations in learning, the vast majority of us have relatively the same potential to max out our genetic potential in intelligence or any other trait that can be altered by a changed environment. The rest of us in the non-genetically influenced 90% can move between a 1 and a 9 depending on how strong or weak our immediate and not-so-immediate environment i

Maybe I can't reach a genetically superior perfect 10 in intelligence, but I'm okay with changing my surroundings to help me reach whatever number I feel comfortable reaching. By the way, 8's and 9's are extremely intelligent. And that level of intelligence, along with many other beneficial Human traits, can be reached by about 90% of our species.

For most of my life, I was okay with my average intelligence and wasn't even close to maxing it out. That is a shame. I was wasting the incredible Human brain I had in my head. I was just waiting. I was waiting for something or somebody else to help me become smarter without really working on it myself, which was another huge waste of time.

{2.8} Most of the greatest accomplishments of our species have been accomplished by the not-so-genetically superior 1-9's, not the genetically gifted 10's. Those Humans who chose to and were able to get their own mind out of the way and let their brain figure things out eventually pushed their way up to a 9. It took a while, but by removing their mind filter and changing their environment, they were able to max out their genetic potential for intelligence and many other traits.

All this means is that nearly every person reading this has the capability of obtaining a high level of intelligence or any other desired human trait (like patience, leadership, long-term vision, confidence, courage, peace, etc.). You and I can become intelligent enough to figure out and fix our own problems. We can become intelligent and courageous enough to deal with whatever life throws at us. We can become intelligent and balanced enough to create and invent things that help or improve our lives and those around us. Intelligent and peaceful enough to become more free than we have ever been.

Your brain. You the reader. Your brain is quite incredible when it comes to figuring things out...

*"So let it. Get out of the way and let it do what it's been doing for a very long time," is what I have to continually tell myself to get my toxic Human mind out of the way to build up my millions-year-old Human brain.*

{2.9} So, how do we maximize our genetic intelligence?

Let's compare two types of brain-mind interactions. Each reader has the ability to make his or her own choice on which brain-mind complex would most likely max out their genetic potential for intelligence and which brain-mind would become more and more of the less-intelligent kind.

## Brain-Mind A

1. was taught to memorize.

2. much information it receives is biasedly filtered by the mind.

3. judges others for their differences.

4. is jealous.

5. is surrounded by a closed-off, restrictive mind.

6. is not open to learning new things.

7. was not exposed to music.

8. was not exposed to the arts.

9. does not recognize connections and/or patterns in anything.

10. only studied/learned a handful of things throughout its life.

11. does not study or try to learn anything it does not agree with.

12. places greater value on getting a paper degree over the skills learned.

13. It is surrounded by a mind that butts into other people 's lives.

14. thinks emotions and feelings are not important.

15. ignores the inner child deep within itself.

16. is surrounded by a "I know-it-all" mind.

17. is accompanied by a closed-mind.

18. devalues long-term in-depth learning and education.

19. makes excuses and blames.

20. struggles with acceptance of those who are different.

**OR...**


### Brain-Mind B

1. was taught how to connect received information to past information.

2. very little information is biasedly filtered by the mind.

3. accepts others for their differences.

4. is not jealous.

5. is surrounded by a free-flowing adaptive mind.

6. is open to learning new things.

7. was exposed to music.

8. was exposed to the arts.

9. does recognize connections and patterns in everything.

10. studied/learned anything and everything throughout its life.

11. studies and tries to learn everything, especially what it does not agree with.

12. places greater value on the skills learned over a paper degree.

13. it is surrounded by a mind that doesn't butt into other people's lives.

14. understands the vast importance of dealing with all emotions and feelings.

15. embraces the inner child deep within itself.

16. is surrounded by a "I know I don't know-it-all" mind.

17. is accompanied by an open-mind.

18. understands the importance of lifelong learning.

19. doesn't know what the words "excuse" or "blame" means :)

20. accepts all, especially who are different from them.

Not a complete list but we get the point. Most of our Human intelligence and many of our Human traits may be more environmentally induced than any other factor. Maybe even more important than the genes passed down by our parents and grandparents. And again, if as a species, we are genetically 99.99% identical, then our brains are mostly the same. But our minds? That's a different story.

It's very likely that our intelligence is much more influenced by the mind surrounding it rather than the genes we were born with.

*What if our Human brains are not the problem? What if it's the Human mind that's the problem?*

# Chapter 3

# Leaving the Path I'm on Behind

{**3.1**} Where do I start? Where do I start rebuilding me? How do I do it? How do I rebuild myself into something that lasts a lifetime? How can I build myself into someone who isn't able to be controlled and manipulated? How do I build myself into someone who can withstand life's challenges while coming back stronger?

*Little by little...*

Having a turtle mentality rather than a rabbit's mentality when it came to rebuilding myself was crucial in achieving real, sustainable change within me. My mind was so weak that I had to start out very small. I knew I had to give myself more time than I would normally give myself. I needed patience. ***Patience can be learned by anyone with a Human brain.*** I knew I could, and I knew I needed a lot of it. I needed to realize that it was going to take time to see real change. I needed to slow down the endless, mostly pointless race I was in.

I needed to leave behind the rabbit's mindset of speeding through everything just to get to the end. "The faster I get to where I want to go, the better, right?"

No, not for me, it just has not worked so far. Same problems over and over. The race was always the same the rabbit's way. Same ending. Same drama, over and over. Same race. There was no way I could keep running this race the same way for my entire life. How boring and pointless...

However, the few times I ran the race using a turtle's mindset, the journey and the endings were always different, new, and exciting. When I ran the race like a rabbit, I didn't plan or adapt or explore different or alternative options, or really cared who I stepped on to get to whatever I wanted.

Many times, others around me were indirectly hurt by my inability to alter my selfish race. The few times I ran the race as a turtle were different; I prepared, I took the time to learn, I adapted as I needed to, I explored new and alternative options, I allowed myself to visualize how things would play out if certain choices were made. I enriched and lifted others around me. It was a completely different life I felt I was living. A whole new, exciting adult world.

So why didn't I continue doing more "turtle races"? I was weak-minded and lazy. It takes real work to accomplish real change. It took questioning myself, my thoughts, my beliefs. It took the ability to accuse myself for the problems in my life, to take more responsibility for my words and actions.

When I raced like a rabbit, I did not have any of those problems to answer to. I just kept racing to the end. Sometimes I won those races, but at what long term cost? Many times, even when I was winning in the short term, the long term cost I was ignoring would come back to bite me.

*Think of when one or more parents put their short term wins of "Having to put my career first" coming back to cause much more long term loss and problems. Subtle, under-the-radar long term damage to the overall development of our kids for the short term gain of our careers.*

{3.2} How would I convert my weak, obsessive, lazy, negative mind into something that wasn't that? I remember the exact place I was when it hit me. I knew how I could convert my toxic mind into something more useful. I finally had enough of my own mind, enough of me, at that point in my life.

It happened after three days of obsessing over a heated conversation I had with a friend. It stopped me cold. I was angry and obsessive for days because of this one conversation. I was angry with the disrespect that happened during the conversation. However, that wasn't the problem. The problem was that I wasted three days of my life obsessing over one conversation. How incredibly dumb! I just stopped as I was walking and bent over in frustration. I yelled as loud as I could to expel the built-up frustration. Frustration and anger of where my mind was. I couldn't believe I wasted days of my life, not hours, but days of my life worrying about how one conversation went. How do I get out of this way of thinking?

I didn't know how but I knew I was ready to try something different. I thought about a few things at this point. 1. The Human brain. 2. Professionals in a variety of fields that have acquired sustained, high levels of success.

My Human brain first. I knew I had to do some rewiring. I knew I had to open up some new channels, new networks, new areas within my brain. I just wasn't sure I could do it. It takes thousands and thousands of hours (8,000-10,000 hours) to fully develop and master a skill or ability in our brain. Or at least a few thousand hours to completely rewrite bad traits and habits. That was originally overwhelming for me to think about and comprehend. However, thousands of hours are made up of single hours, which are made up of minutes, which are made up of seconds. I started there.

I started low too. I changed my weak mind and my destructive thoughts 30 seconds at a time. That was about as long as my mind could last until it would wander off into something bad. I would bring it back 30 seconds at a time. I knew if I could think of something good and productive for seconds, then I would eventually be able to do them for several minutes, then more minutes, then hours, then days, then weeks, months, etc.

And that's exactly how it played out. I changed my thoughts and mind 30 seconds at a time until my physical brain was making long term connections. Those 30 second intervals would turn into minutes-long intervals of me having a productive, non-toxic adult mind. Eventually as those minutes became hours, weeks, months, and years, they became me. There is no question to me anymore about mind and brain development. Our brain and mind will become whatever we primarily feed into it. A lot of our own personal life boils down to what thoughts and behaviors we give priority to.

***We become what we dominate our minds and brain with.***

{3.3} I needed some solid, productive tasks to do, to distract my mind from being unproductive and toxic during these rewiring sessions. I found it helped so much to jump into a project, chore, hobby, or something I was interested in that contained small parts. Something small that required full attention from my eyes, ears, hands, mind, and brain. Something that would cause my mind to slow the constant running and the constant negativity.

*This is when I started having real, unbiased, deep conversations with myself. I would talk to myself like I was talking to a friend sharing advice with one another. I would tell myself that it was okay to get angry and frustrated, it's natural. But the obsession is not natural or normal. It's counterproductive and wastes precious time. I only have one chance at this life, why am I wasting so much time on things that do not matter?*

I finally understood why Bonsai trees are so popular within some Asian cultures. Caring for them and pruning them is very tedious. They have very small leaves. Pruning each tiny leaf takes much focus and concentration. That focused concentration breaks those obsessive, unproductive thoughts. It gives the mind a break and allows the brain to do what it does best. Observe and learn and solve!

If I couldn't get my hands on something physical, I would still use small visual distractions. The smaller, the better. For me, it would work well to break my never-ending time-wasting thoughts. I remember this one time when I was deep into self-pity and time-wasting thoughts. I picked up a leaf from a tree and stared at it. I stared and focused on the tiniest features that I could. The numerous veins, the different shapes, the tiniest color variations, the imperfections. Anything to divert my mind and allow my brain to start the rewiring process. I was willing to do whatever I needed to do to change my mind and my brain.

These new techniques were all uncomfortable at first. Very awkward and uncomfortable. I felt stupid doing some of these things, but I knew I needed to try something different. I had to. I was not wasting my life on this planet. I was tired of the path I was going down. I was tired of being held back by others. I was ready to leave behind the people that were holding me back.

*I needed to find the person inside of me that wouldn't allow others to hold me back anymore.*

{3.4} Little by little, second by second, minute by minute, things started to change. The patience I was developing was crucial since this could take several months to several years. I was able to stop and stay out of those toxic, wasteful thoughts for longer and longer periods of time. My thoughts started becoming more productive. My focus was sharpening. My <u>core</u> <u>personality trait</u>—made up of <u>unnecessary and excessive worrying</u> about things in my life that did not matter or I couldn't control—was starting to crack.

Now that I had more control over my mind, it was time to start the next phase of rewiring my brain. I had to build up my own self-worth and a strong, unwavering inner confidence. Since low self-worth and weak, erratic inner confidence was the root of so many of my problems, they had to be fixed.

But where to begin? I turned my attention to people with sustained success. Those with sustained success most likely wouldn't have long periods of their life dominated with low levels of confidence. They probably wouldn't have weak, erratic confidence either. I watched and learned. I unbiasedly watched and learned. I observed the greats from many different areas of life. The great athletes, the great artists, the great musicians, the great entertainers, the great teachers, the great plumbers, etc.

What was sustained success? Most of us, professional or not, great in our field or not, will have a bad year, down season, bad performance, poor piece, bad day. That's normal. Even the best of the best have had bad "performances" from time to time. But for the most part, those with sustained success usually had long, productive, rewarding careers. They may have had a bad season, or bad album, or a bad piece here and there but over the life of their career, they stayed somewhere near the top of their profession. The opposite of that are teams or individuals that win or produce great pieces or performances rarely, surrounded by many mediocre or average results. They are rarely at the top of their profession for an extended period of time. They become more dependent on one-hit wonders or very few go-to skills. They are usually full of inconsistent results.It didn't make much sense. We are all so similar. Why are so few of us consistently successful? We all have the same 24 hours in a day. Right? But...but the lifelong success-ful ones were not lacking in inner confidence and self-worth.Those individuals who figured out how to reach and keep a high level of success were not much different biologically or genetically than the individuals who did not achieve long-term success. It really wasn't physical or genetic differences that separated the long-term successful ones from the rarely successful ones. It was, as usual, the state of mind that was the key.

So, what's the difference? To me, it was a perspective differ-ence. There were obviously several factors involved in making their long-term success possible. However, we will focus on the ones per-taining to us. The main point is that I didn't have to possess special inherited genes to be great at something. I didn't need to be born into a rich family or community. It almost became simple. I could be great at anything in life that I wanted. I also could be great at many things in life, not just one or two. I didn't need money to be great. I didn't need degrees to be great. I didn't need to be a celebrity or a famous athlete to be great. As long as I changed my perspective into something realistic and productive, I could be a dominant, in-control badass in many areas of my life.

There was a common thread among the greats across different disciplines. Most of them were masters of the fundamentals of their craft. There was a clear difference in perspective and focus when it came down to mastering the absolute basics of their skills. Over and over, the ones who were consistently at the top of their field ferociously worked on getting better by pushing themselves to learn new, challenging techniques while never ever stopping their work on the basic fundamentals of their craft.

*Individuals and teams at this point could be substituted with families. There are many similarities between long term successful teams/individuals and successful families. And most of the long term successful families I witnessed were not sustainably successful because of money or inherited traits. They were successful because of their healthy, realistic perspectives on life.*

The teams, individuals, or families that were *not* consistently at the top of their profession or life continually regarded the "basic fundamentals" of anything...*beneath them*. They did the bare minimum to get by. They focused more on fancy, advanced, materialistic, superficial crowd-loving techniques. For families, they tended to follow the latest, fancy trends (new diets, new fashion trends, new ways to learn, etc.), without putting much effort into "mastering the basic fundamentals" of life. Their success was inconsistent. They became too dependent on others for their own success. They became dependent on landing the "next big thing" that would change their life for the better. As these families or individuals waited around for their next big break, they usually failed to continually work on improving any of their basic, fundamental life skills. So, their basic life skills eroded while they waited for something to happen. This did not happen to long-term successful professionals and families. They did not let their basic, fundamental skills erode. They all continually maintained and worked on those skills.

It does not matter about our physical limitations. It does not matter about our genetic makeup. It comes down to if our minds will allow us to work on something for a long enough period of time to master and dominate it. Despite a few obvious and not-so-obvious physical or genetic limitations in each of us, most of us can dominate and master many different areas of our life. Remember, it takes a few thousand hours to get to a level of high comfortability. If we stop after the 1000th hour, then we will never see what we have to offer at hour 4000 or hour 8000.

It takes several years to get enough hours to reach that level. It's a process that's frustrating and difficult, but very rewarding and exciting. When we allow our brain to put in the hours and hours of building and neural networking, it will, in turn, build a stronger, more complex problem-solving brain that reveals its true hidden talents. This is when we get to higher levels of understanding and intelligence. It's like getting to the expert level of brain development. Your understanding becomes deep and thorough enough that you can see how things play out before they happen. You can problem-solve quickly. New channels open up deep in your brain. New connections are made. Senses become stronger and better connected to one another. Things that used to be fast and confusing become slower and clearer. Higher level mind and brain functioning ensues.

However, there is a trick about "just" getting to 8000-10,000 hours. It requires a little more than just physical repetition. You can do something over and over for thousands of hours but still have limited knowledge of how things are working on a deeper level. We must challenge the brain to keep learning on the edge of frustration.

*Behind pain and frustration are the answers to many of our questions and problems. That's where physical growth (muscle getting bigger after pushing them to levels of pain and frustration) and mental growth (building inner confidence and inner well-being) occurs. The key to our answers about our lives are in the places we don't want to go.*

Repetition alone does not get the brain to higher levels of functioning. Many challenges, mistakes, failures, and rebounds within those repetitions get us there. Continual learning of the nuanced details of our craft will allow for the building of new channels and new connections within our brain.

Those that I observed that were successful long-term had another thing in common. They loved learning old and new things about their craft. They continued making connections between old and new information. They were not afraid of making mistakes. They did not prioritize their own image and own selfish needs. They understood and embraced the challenge of controlling their own minds while restricting the lazy, selfish, my-needs-first type of mindset. They eventually or maybe, earlier than most of us, figured out how to navigate their way through the Human mind as a way to enhance themselves and others around them rather than letting the Human mind guide them deep into the patterned pitfalls of Human life.

{3.5} How do I translate the long-term success of professionals to my personal life? What are the basic fundamentals of life? What would I become if I became a master of the basic fundamentals of being a Human? I had to find out; my curiosity was exploding. I wanted and needed to see what I would become if I played the game of life differently—better, smarter—while being much less dependent on others.

I figured if I continued down the same relatively simple path I felt I was going down, which was pretty much following the advice of people around me, my life would end up like those around me; stuck with nowhere to go and highly dependent on others. Did I really want my life to become what others wanted it to be?

I didn't know what I wanted, really. I mostly only knew what other people wanted me to be like. I just knew I wanted a different type of life. But I was lacking enough confidence to make any real changes. *The urge to be accepted by others around me was overwhelming.* I was scared of being labeled a nerd or a loser because I was doing or thinking something that wasn't generally accepted by the others around me. Something as easy as reading a book or eating healthy food in front of them was excruciatingly painful because of the fear of rejection. For most of my life I chose to be accepted by the people around me rather than educating myself, taking care of my own health, or becoming more intellectually independent. I would always give into the pressure of being accepted. I was so weak!

Again, I watched, listened, and learned. Which individuals or families had lifelong success? Success like those professionals? Success at life that was attainable, sustainable, learnable, and teachable. Were there patterns?

...oh yeah, plenty.

The following are the characteristics I was continually finding in lifelong successful families and individuals:

### *Patterns of the Successful*

1. Highly open-minded home.
2. Adaptable to changes in their lives.
3. Had more self-created ups than downs.

4. Their downs were infrequent as well as shorter in duration.

5. Were able to healthily recover from those downs, even severe ones.

6. Lacked drama and chaos.

7. Lacked lying and cheating.

8. All possessed a healthy level of confidence.

9. There was a lot of freedom to be yourself.

10. High degree of accepting others who are different.

### *Patterns of the Unsuccessful*

1. Highly close-minded home.

2. Struggled with adapting to changes in their life.

3. Had more self-created downs than ups.

4. Their downs occurred more frequently and the duration lasted for longer periods of time.

5. Slow recovery from the lows of life.

6. Continuous and consistent chaos and drama in their life.

7. Consistent lying and cheating.

8. Most possessed a low level of confidence.

9. Very little to zero freedom to be yourself.

10. Very little acceptance of others who are different.

Where would I start? Where would I start trying to change my life if I'm at the bottom and seemingly stuck in a never ending downward cycle? I had no money, no resources, and no one who really cared. Where do I go? Where do I start?

Within. I went within. I went within me. I didn't need much to fix the basic, fundamental problems I had in my own life. I didn't need money to fix my problems. I didn't need anybody else. I needed me. Open-mindedness, adapting to change, consistent maintenance of self, surrounded by lifelong learning were key differences between the consistently successful and the unsuccessful. They didn't take money or help from anybody else. I could do those myself no matter how poor or low I go.

It did take common sense, however. Something I was lacking and needed to build. It also took doing things differently than the majority of people around me. I had to learn how to do the things that worked, not what was popular.

So, what were the basic fundamentals of life that I needed to "master"? What did I need to do to become proficient in order to build my own self-worth and inner confidence, as well as lessen my dependence on others?

As usual, I started small, very small. I started with basic personal maintenance. Not only was creating a productive, secure personal living space important, but creating a personal space that was easy to maintain over many years became more important. It's almost pointless to set up a new personal space if after only a few months I would fall back into the same old habits of not maintaining and letting things get away from me and returning to the same old life with the same old problems.

*For example, I could buy a whole new bedroom set, reorganize my closets, and paint my walls a new color. But, if I don't learn how to consistently maintain them, the same problems will eventually show up. Clutter will slowly start to fill the same areas as before. Even though I had a nice new room, I still had never learned any kind of basic, fundamental organizational skills. And as always, the same old problems would show up because of my disorganization.*

That example of a new bedroom not being able to be consistently maintained reminds me of most of my relationships. I would get into a new relationship hoping things would change for the better and be better than the previous relationship. That rarely happened because I never learned the basic, common sense fundamentals of relationships. Same clutter would show up in the same places.

Before I tackled the main issues, I practiced taming the milder, more simpler ones. Before I fully went into figuring out what my deep mental issues were, I worked on things that would give me a more immediate sense of accomplishment. I needed momentum. I was nowhere close to being ready to tackle the worst parts of my personality. But I knew I could slowly build my inner confidence by working on my smaller problems.

Figuring out and defeating smaller problems in my life led to more little victories. Those little victories carried me to and through to the next problem I would eventually tackle. If I could figure out and solve one little problem, why not two, why not three?

I started in my bedroom, my immediate personal space. A space, if created properly, would be a comfortable, secure place where I could lift myself up, lick my wounds, and regain strength and confidence both physically and mentally.

I did not have that kind of personal space to go to. Not even close. I have a neat house and neat bedroom, always have, but there's a difference between a kept-up neat house that's not efficiently functional and a house that is thoughtfully and efficiently laid out. Some homes can enhance your life while some homes can suck the life out of you. I was neat but not efficiently organized. Lots of wasted time looking for stuff. So many other things in my life were so much more important to me than setting up my living area properly. I was so wrong. In the long-run, because of my own inefficient disorganization, I lost so much time and energy while unintentionally creating a life-sucking personal space.

I was doing that to myself. No more! No more of this waste! I decided to take as much time as I needed to reorganize my personal space. I planned things out in a way that was very comfortable, secure, and efficiently organized. I wasn't much of a planner so it did take some time to figure out what I wanted to do. I played out several different setups in my head before I started. But once I figured out in my head what I could do with my personal space, the pressure and stress of reorganizing my bedroom seemed to go away. Also, it didn't take much time out of my life to reorganize. I put that off for years dreading the time it would take out of my life to do something so boring and meaningless. Dumb. Really dumb.

After only a few days, I had transformed my personal space into something that would lift me, not sink me. The time I spent doing personal chores dropped dramatically. It became fun to finally be able to dominate my personal space while gaining many hours of extra time over the course of each month.

I asked myself these questions while I was playing with the different setups in my head. Which would I feel best in when I enter my room? Which would save me the most time? Which would replenish me the most?

I was creating something for myself by myself. It felt great. I could set up my space like I wanted without input from others. No matter how crazy life was getting I always had a secure, comfortable personal space to go back to.

Like I mentioned above, the time I spent doing personal chores was cut drastically. Along with the higher degree of organization came a loss of wasted time and a gain of more time to do other things that I would rather be doing. Instead of my usual bitching and complaining about the never-ending chores, I decided to master them by minimizing their dominance over my life. I spent way too many disorganized, wasted hours on picking up after myself. Not anymore.

Thirty minutes down to five minutes for just one chore: putting away laundry. I gained 25 free minutes on one chore. I sure wish I figured out common sense, efficient organization a long time ago. Confidence and extra time gained. Now we are off to a good start. I was starting to slowly build a stronger, more dynamic brain and mind by "mastering" the very basics of life. Continual maintenance of myself, which includes my personal space, is one of the basic fundamentals of life.

{3.6} The way we organize our physical world can give us insight into how our brains and minds are organizing themselves. The physical, material things that I either forgot were there or intentionally chose not to remember were there slowly, but surely, started to build up in the neglected, unmaintained corners of my room. This was most likely how I built the foundation of how my brain organizes the information I put into it.

I did have those thoughts, feelings, or problems that I left neglected and unmaintained in the deep corners of my brain and mind. What would happen if I cleaned out, reorganized, and maintained those deep corners in my house? What about in my brain and mind?

Would it have similar effects? In my organized, maintained room, those once-neglected corners became usable space. I also had more time to do other things. Would my brain be able to use more of itself just like my room? Would I gain more time and more space in my own brain by applying the same basic fundamentals that I applied to my room? I had to find out...

Real change takes years. I knew that, so I needed many small things to work on while the big changes were slowly being created "behind the scenes."

The physical reorganization of the brain worked really well for me. I could work on the easier physical, external organization of my life while slowly rewiring my brain. I also didn't have to face the deep corners of my brain...yet. That was very good for me. I didn't have enough confidence built up yet to face my true personality flaws or fears. Not yet anyway.

I worked through my entire house after redoing my personal space. Drawer by drawer, closet by closet, room by room.

1. **Clear out**

2. **Get rid of**

3. **Reorganize**

4. **Maintain**

Again and again, area by area, room by room. If I didn't need it, use it, or if it just wasted time or space, it had to go. However, above all, over and over again, it became crystal clear: if I wasn't willing to maintain the work I did, it would always return to the previous state of wasted time and space.

*No maintenance equals no long-term gain. Consistent maintenance, not obsessive maintenance, is one of the truest, most influential fundamental basics of our species.*

I was pretty sure, even at this point, that our minds and brains would need to be maintained on a regular consistent basis.

As for the consistently long-term successful Humans, they proved over and over that they were masters at common sense, logical maintenance of their personal hygiene, their own health, their personal space, their self-made abilities and skills, and of course their minds and brains. They did not let things go unmaintained for years and years (weeks or months maybe), but not years.

Most of us will go through challenging times that will erode our ability to sufficiently maintain our life. That is perfectly normal and perfectly okay. None of us should be expected to be machines and always be on top of everything. That's an unfair and an unrealistic way to live. Sometimes we have to go down a little bit. That's not the problem. It's staying down for too long. When I would stay down for too long while not maintaining the basics of my life, the recovery and rebound time was drastically longer and much more difficult, like a job loss, loss of family, major illness, etc. It was so much harder to come back from life's challenges if I also had an unmaintained personal life and space.

I personally think consistent, common sense maintenance of one's life is one of the greatest weapons we can use against the dark corners of our species. The dark, neglected corners in my brain and mind started to resemble those areas in my house. When those neglected, unmaintained corners were left to grow, eventually the unorganized, "I'll deal with it later" mess left the corner and started invading other areas of my room. The problem areas that I was once able to hide and ignore started spilling over into new areas of my room. I would lose my comforting, secure, life-enhancing personal space. I lost myself.

For me it worked like this: when I felt like I was slipping into a dark corner of life, I would use the simple organization of my personal space to dampen the blows.

*A Human brain with hope and excitement is a forever creative, exciting, problem-solving brain. A Human brain that lacks hope and excitement is a forever dark, mapless, lost brain.*

{**3.7**} I couldn't believe it worked, time and time again. When I focused on maintaining myself, my most natural needs became clear. No matter if I had a crushing blow, like a career loss or the loss of a relationship, turning the attention to myself and going back to maintaining the most basic areas of my Human needs helped me recover faster and healthier (like not obsessing over it for too long).

Taking time to step back, reevaluate things while giving myself enough time to reflect on what I have done to put myself in these repeated situations. This was new to me. I would normally just jump into a new relationship or new job while blaming everything and anything for my loss.

During which, several months or years would go by and maintaining the basics of my life would fall by the wayside. Then I would lose myself in the new job or new relationship. Similar patterns and problems would eventually start to creep up. Again and again, new job, new relationship, same old problems. Same old problems to go along with a massive mountain of unmaintained basics of my Human life. My health would deteriorate. I ate more, ate worse, exercised less, blamed more, made more excuses, neglected personal space, etc. Those unkempt corners would eventually take over my entire "house."

I did not mind being down for a short period of time. I liked giving myself time to deal with loss or the lows of life. Just a reasonable amount of time though. I gave myself time to explore any and all emotions and feelings that came up. I believe it makes any of us immensely more powerful within if we don't run away from our feelings and emotions. If I knew where my feelings were, what triggered them, and how to control them when they decided to show up, I figured it would make my life a little easier and a little more manageable.

I figured there haven't been many in our species that have managed to do this. First off, it's incredibly challenging. Second, many of our species deny the importance of recognizing, dealing with, and using feelings and emotions. Thirdly, there's a harsh judgment we put upon those who do recognize and use their feelings and emotions. Most of us have always been told how unimportant feelings and emotions are. I've heard from many of us who think that having feelings and emotions make us weaker. There are few things more ignorant and stupid than that way of thinking. Those among us who have explored the depths of our emotions and feelings, that go along with our strengths and weaknesses, are always stronger than those of us who do not.

The strongest among us that I have observed are not the ones who deny or ridicule emotions and feelings. They are the ones who embrace the importance and power that understanding, feeling, and control of their emotions can bring. They allow themselves to be sad, remorseful, happy, peaceful, loving, caring, and more depending on the situation. They don't waste time, however, with emotions like hate, anger, jealousy, and judgment. Those simply make us dumber. Hate, anger, jealousy, and judgment are rarely used by highly successful Humans. These will bring any Human life down with them. The mind and brain of Humans who hate and judge other Humans who are different from them are closed and neglected. It's impossible to use large areas of our brains and minds if it is cluttered with hate, anger, jealousy, and judgment. These emotions program our brains and minds to disregard usable information. Having hate, anger, jealousy, and judgment as part of our personality will guarantee a life full of misery, problems, loss, and missed opportunities.

Many of the greatest professionals I observed would go back to the basics of their craft to reset. If they were in a rut, not playing or performing up to their standards, they reset. They went back to the most basic of skills. It was a little weird at first watching those great professionals practicing first-level (elementary) skills. Basketball players practicing footwork, football players practicing tackling or blocking, award-winning musicians working with very basic skills (like working on basic timing).

As awkward as it was to watch some of the all-time greats doing basic kid-like drills, it worked for them. Over and over again, it worked. They were performing maintenance on their basic, fundamental skills that they neglected for too long. Everything worthwhile needs maintenance (our mind, our brain, our personality, our homes, etc.). When they ignored the maintenance of their basic skills, their advanced skills would also diminish. Remember, most advanced skills originate from basic, fundamental skills. So, when those greats reset, and went back to maintaining their core basic skills, they quickly rebounded and rose back to the higher levels that they were accustomed to.

The same goes for the management and maintenance of our personal lives. The longer we stay away from the basics of being a Human, the more our basic and advanced skills will erode. But once we get comfortable in the continuous maintenance of us and our lives, resetting ourselves becomes easier and easier. We also give ourselves a way to get out of the challenging lows of life. It's a great tool to use to reset our life.

{3.8} The more I cleared, faced, and dominated the neglected areas of my home, the clearer my mind and brain became. I may have not been ready at that point to face my deep personality flaws, but I could feel I was headed in the right direction.

Before tackling any new project, like dealing with a neglected part of my house, anxiety and stress would kick in. Many times I would start, then give up or not start at all. I needed a new strategy. Much of my fear and anxiety came from not knowing what to do with all the stuff I've been ignoring, whether in my head or my house.

I started with the physical house first. I gave myself several options. I could throw away, recycle, donate, keep, give away, or sell. As I pulled something out, it would have several places that it could go. I liked the flexibility of having multiple options. It kept me from being boxed into one or two options. When it came to keeping things, I had to have common sense, intellectual plans. If I did not use something for a year or more, it most likely needed to go. If it made my life more challenging, took too much time, energy, or space, it had a good chance of leaving. I wanted to simplify and maximize my time and space. Material things can clutter, a lot. I loved buying new things; it made me feel happy. But if I didn't know how or didn't want to keep up with the new things that I bought, most likely, and eventually, another neglected corner would start to form.

My brain and my mind would eventually flourish from doing this. I would definitely say, for me, there is a strong, deep connection between my physical, external environment and the deep functions of my brain and mind. With each drawer, with each closet, with each room that I cleared and organized, my mind and brain became clearer and clearer. There was little doubt to me anymore that some of the dark, neglected corners of my brain were decluttering and reorganizing in tandem with what I was doing in my physical, personal space. I had to learn this over and over to make it stick. Just like I had to continually maintain my personal, physical space, I had to continually maintain and declutter my mind and brain. *Maintenance baby!*

I used a wide variety of "tricks" and "techniques" to focus and refocus my wandering mind. Many times my weak, wandering mind wanted to do anything else. I would tell myself to "just work on it for 30 minutes, to get a good start, and then stop if you want to." I put no pressure and no timeframe when rebuilding myself. I also wanted to *complete* things I started, which in turn would build more confidence.

Strict timeframes and rigid schedules did not work for me when I was rebuilding myself. I somewhat gave myself a loose decade to figure myself out. I was not about to put a time limit on learning how to build myself. I really did not care how long it took. I just knew where I wanted to be.

I would also start with the easier tasks first. I also started with the tasks that I could complete relatively fast. Our brains thrive on completing something it starts. It loves to see things through to the end, especially when smaller completions occur from the beginning. Once we give our brains a little bit of momentum, watch what happens. It's incredible.

If my mind was really toxic and lazy on a particular project and it was trying to get me to do anything else than what I should be doing, I would shut it down. I would yell at myself sometimes. I would scold myself. I would tell myself, "Let's just do it for 30 minutes, that's it." And then, "If you can't do something for just 30 minutes, how strong of a person can we really be?" Anything to get my stupid mind to start doing something productive!

For example, if I was working on a room (20 feet by 20 feet) to declutter and reorganize, my toxic mind would start focusing on the total project. It would focus on how much time it would take to do it. It would focus on how boring it would be to do this. My mind would even make the case that I'm too cool to do a project like this, "What if somebody I knew saw me doing this?" Excuse after excuse. It was constantly trying to figure a way out. This was a major flaw in my personality.

My brain however, unlike my mind, was trying to focus on only one small area of the room. So, I told my wasteful mind to "shut the hell up" for a little while and let the brain do its thing. I then just focused on one shelf in one small area of the room. I did not care about the entire room at this point. I just planned on how to tackle that one shelf, then I would begin to plan the rest of the room. My brain was allowed to focus on the one task at hand, nothing else. It focused on what would be the most efficient way to organize just one shelf. It also found a good starting point to go along with the all-important end-point. You start with this one shelf, you end with that one shelf. You complete that short, relatively simple task, from start to finish. Completing something you start is huge, no matter how small.

I would then focus on a small area of the room next. I would tackle and complete just a small five foot by five foot area instead of the entire 20 by 20 foot area. Those completed shelves were in those smaller areas. To start an area that already has something finished within it can be a huge boost to productivity and confidence.

It helps to know what gets each of our brains going or what turns it off. It'll be different for each of us. This is where knowing yourself intimately really pays off. I knew some of my weaknesses and some of my strengths at this point. My weakness was getting started. I was a procrastinator. I did complete much of which I started but I mostly rushed through things and took the easy way out. Most of these completions were superficial and did not build a better brain. Just completing something that I started wasn't enough. I had to give myself enough time to learn how to complete it the right way. When I did allow myself the time to do it the right way, I encountered much less problems later on. Rushing through a task or job just to complete it does not work.

*Taking shortcuts in brain-building will result in a less-than brain that can be easily manipulated.*

Rewiring and rebuilding the Human brain is not easy. I gave myself a lot of time when I was allowing my brain to learn about efficient organization. If I took the time to effectively learn how to efficiently organize my personal space to maximize my time, my brain used that time to rebuild and rewire itself. At first it was pretty slow. It took me a while to figure out an efficient way of organizing my space. But eventually our brain will be so good at it, we will be able to organize and maintain our space at high levels in a fraction of the time it used to take. Anything that takes time and is hard in the beginning will eventually become easier and quicker. I had to start somewhere. I did not care anymore how long it would take.

*I couldn't wait to see what my brain had to offer! I created for myself a never-ending, ever-exciting, forever-surprising lifelong journey! And it's all in my own head!*

{**3.9**} Now I was ready to explore other areas of my life that I wanted to become more independent in. I wanted and needed to become more independent in other areas in my life. I also knew I wanted my independence to enhance my life goals. Did I want to live to an old age? Did I want to be active when I was at that old age? How much dependency on others was I comfortable with as I aged?

**Each one of us has the Human Right to live our life the way we want, not what someone else wants. Each one of us has the right to choose whatever we want our personal diet to be. Each one of us has the right to develop whatever kind of body we like. Each one of us has the right to live to whatever age we want to and design our life around that. No other Human has the right to tell another Human how or who to be.**

I wanted to live to an old age and I wanted to be active and healthy when I was there. But that's my personal goal. Everyone has the right to choose their own. That goal of mine helped make the way I live my life easier. My decision making started to clear up after I started to figure out how I wanted my life to play out. My long term vision started to kick in as well. But again, there is nothing wrong with choosing a shorter life and playing the game differently.

For me, I'm curious. I'm curious about what happens to Earth while I'm here. I'm also really curious to see what this Human brain and mind of mine has to offer.

I was not comfortable with being dependent on others for my well-being as I aged. I needed to be able to take care of as much as I could in regards to my own health. I needed to feel comfortable with developing a plan for preventing as many modern chronic diseases as I could. I needed to form a plan to master the basics of my own health. I was not trying to replace my doctors. I just wanted to understand how to take care of my own health most of the time.

In fact, I expanded the types of doctors that I used. I sought the opinion of as many different types of medical minds that I could. I now take the advice and opinions of several doctors, not one. I would seek the advice of Allopathic (modern) doctors, Naturopathic doctors (natural methods), and Functional doctors (uses natural and modern methods). Why limit my options to the opinion of doctors from only one type of healing method, one type of mindset?

Doctors who are close minded are not open to a variety of healing methods. I stayed away from those types. I would ask myself, "If something works to heal my body and doesn't cause long-term damage, then why does it matter what kind of doctor it comes from?"

Doctors are Humans just like the rest of us, and they can fall into the same species pitfalls we all do. Doctors who are not open to learning and trying new, old and different methods are dangerous and mostly a waste of my time. They can only take your health so far, as they quickly run out of options for how to treat you. Their success rates tend to be lower than open minded doctors who kept learning new, old, and different methods of healing. They were more adaptable and had more options to use. They were comfortable with going out of their comfort zone and trying new things, even if they were not taught that in medical school. I had much greater success with those types of doctors in all fields of medicine.

What about the other times when I probably could have handled my medical situation without depending on a doctor? If I would have kept up with trying to learn how to keep myself healthy, I wouldn't be so dependent on others for my health now.

I had to figure it out for myself. What habits could I develop that would slowly make me become less dependent on others? I was also done with fad-type, the what's-popular-now diet and exercise programs. Most did not work or did not last for me. While learning how to heal myself, I decided I might as well learn some good fall-back diets and exercises. Could I figure out a lifelong diet and exercise plans that I was comfortable with? I needed one or a few to go back to and use to reset my health. I knew I wasn't always going to be perfect so I needed something that would be able to keep my health from falling too low. I had to find out. It also needed to fit my lifestyle. I needed something that was effective, safe, and had long-term benefits, while also being built by common sense and intellect. I told myself, "Take time with this. Explore and try as many options as we can. There is no rush. Let's take years if we need to. We could basically only spend the next 3-5 years figuring out a lifelong diet and exercise plan that would last several decades. Not a bad trade-off."

You should absolutely develop your own methods that are different from mine. Yours will be custom fit to you, your lifestyle, your life-goals, your desired long-term self-image, and your schedule. However, you can use any or all of my methods if you like and modify them to your style.

I have tried many different methods. I use a variety of them throughout the year depending on the season and my obligations. My diet and exercises change with the seasons. Keeps it fresher and easier. Eating foods in season especially helps. I started with and kept a wide open mind throughout the entire process. I tried things I was not comfortable with or have always hated or looked down upon when it came to different foods and exercises.

{3.10} Take exercise for example. There are so many different ways to exercise. I started small and analyzed the basics of our species health. What was the minimum I could do to keep my overall health from plummeting? If I was hit by a particularly stressful time in my life and there was no way in hell that I could keep up with my health, were there simple, common sense, intellectual things I could do during that time to keep my health from falling too low?

*"Think and act like a turtle, not like a rabbit," I would tell myself when needed.*

I thought, what were some subtle small things that I could do to enhance my overall physical and mental health? What if I could work them into my daily life? Were some of the subtleties in my current everyday life enhancing or inhibiting my long-term health?

For example, when I looked at the top five reasons for deaths in the Western World (United States, Mexico, Central America, South

America), I found four out of the top five to be preventable. The one that was not preventable was accidents. One other one is cancer while the other three deal with the cardiovascular system: heart attacks, strokes, aneurysms, etc

Like we previously talked about, most cancers are preventable. Upwards of 90% of cancers are non-genetic. Genetic-based cancers (non-environmental) make up small portions of any population of any species, about 5-10%. The DNA molecule makes very few replicating mistakes (one in a billion). Also, genetic-based cancers have been around since the first cells started dividing billions of years ago. Cancer can be found in any living thing that has cells that divide. Plants get cancer, birds get cancer, fungus gets cancer. We have found dinosaurs with remnants of brain cancer within their skulls. Genetic defects rarely run rampant through a species. They do not run rampant through ours either. The "it's my genes" excuse can only be applied to a very small percentage of us in our species.

The replication process of DNA in all living cells is simply spectacular in its efficiency. When our cells divide, there is less than one chance in a billion that a mistake is made when copying the genetic information. It's more efficient with its accuracy than supercomputers. Most of our species' chronic diseases are not caused by our genetics. They are caused by the internal and external environments we have created.

I now believe, because I did not used to, that it's totally possible, if not somewhat simple, to avoid the top four killers in the Western World. We'll come back to cancer in a bit.

For now, what about cardiovascular diseases? The heart and its associated blood vessels. From the start, I asked myself, "What's the most basic principle of the heart and blood vessels?" I immediately thought of engines. I was still rookie-like with my knowledge of engines, but I did know one basic principle of keeping them running for many years. Don't let them sit.

Same with us and any living thing that has anything flowing continuously through them. If the flow slows down, things (cells, organs) will not work properly. A surefire way to get a top five killer cardiovascular disease is to sit more than we move. More sitting, less flow. Less flow, more problems...continual problems. Just like engines, we are built to move.

Not moving more than moving was setting me up to die early like many others in the Western World. And of course, the opposite is true as well. If I continually moved throughout the day more than I sat, I was already adding years to my life while preventing many life-shortening diseases. I'm not even to the exercising and dieting part yet. This is just moving and walking around. Pretty simple start for me. Common sense baby!

I didn't need a doctor to help me move either. That was all on me. At a minimum, I would move (walk) for 10 minutes every 50 minutes. Even if I was sitting more than moving at this ratio, the health benefits were already greater than not doing this. Of everything I have read and researched on this, that was the baseline of pretty much the least we could do to maintain some level of healthy blood flow through our hearts and blood vessels.

**_Even my engines last longer now since I run them more than they sit!_**

Even cancers struggle with consistent, strong blood flow. As bad as cancers are, they have weaknesses. And we can intelligently prevent most of them by using common sense. I started my learning by removing my self-derived biases, beliefs, and ideas. Then I observed, researched, and learned unbiasedly!

- Cancers do not like oxygen. Oxygen is found in flowing blood.
- Cancers like bodies with weak immune systems.
- Cancers love certain types of sugar.

Over the last few million years, our immune systems have developed sophisticated ways to fight off many diseases, from viruses to bacteria to fungi, as well as many cancers. We are born equipped with cancer-killing cells. Over the first two decades of our life, we built an extensive and impressive variety of methods to defend against many of our internal problems. From inflammation, bad bacteria, virus, acute and chronic diseases, to cancers, our body's immune system is well equipped to handle it. Then when we are in our early 20s, we build and manufacture yet another group of cancer-killing cells. All the cancer-killing cells we have actively seek out and try to destroy any cancer cell that it encounters.

Why would I take that ability away from our millions-year-old immune system? If it's been battling and conquering diseases and cancers for that long, then I should be enhancing it, not inhibiting it.

If I develop and build a weak immune system that isn't capable of proper defense against many diseases, including cancers, they then become able to set up shop and stay in us for a very long time, causing long-term problems. A weak human immune system gets many acute (short-term) *and* chronic (long-term) diseases. A strong human immune system gets very few of either. Diseases caused from either bad bacteria, viruses, chronic inflammation, or cancer are all like predators looking for weak prey they can control and consume. They are looking for weaknesses in an environment that lacks the ability to defend itself from attack. We have so much control over the performance of our own immune system. The first 22 years of our life sets the stage for how our immune system will perform through the next several decades. Our immune systems usually mature by our early 20s.

*We have immense control over the long-term performance of our immune systems.*

Another weakness of cancer is its love of sugar. Sugar is its fuel. Sugar on cancer is gas on fire. Not all sugars are fuel to cancers though. Some sugars and their components can actually inhibit some cancers. More on that in a bit.

But first, let's look at the common sense problems associated with too many sugars in us. Besides cancer, certain sugars (not all sugars are bad) and certain amounts of sugars can have disastrous effects on many other systems, especially the cardiovascular system. Let's just start with the basics of sugar. When we spill a sugary drink on the counter, what does it feel like? It's sticky. Certain sugars and high amounts of those certain sugars can and eventually do become sticky within our blood vessels and heart. What would happen to the blood flow if the blood became stickier? Blood flow slows. Less oxygen and less food get to our cells. Our cells all over our body may slowly start to struggle. They cannot be expected to perform at high levels if they are receiving less than what they are used to. Those cells furthest away from your heart will begin to struggle first.; toes, fingers, feet, hands. I then looked up diabetic feet to get the full visual effect on what the end result of this was. Green and black toes and feet. Slow blood flow slowly killed all those cells in the toes and feet, and in some cases, legs from knees down were lost. And what are diabetics known for? Too much sugar in the blood. Just because we can't see the subtle, everyday effects of our actions (good or bad) doesn't mean something isn't happening deep, deep within our bodies.

*Good or bad, consistent habits make us or break us over the course of our life.*

If I would sit more and move less, combined with too many bad sugars in my blood, I would be able to comfortably predict that my life would end much earlier than it should, accompanied by many health problems.

Just by walking and moving more than not moving would at least help to minimize the damage done by a high-sugar, sedentary lifestyle. Also, I was not about to build my life around foods that would have a long-term negative affect on my health.

Next, I needed to figure out what sugars (carbs), fats, and proteins were harmful to the human body, and which were essential and helpful to the human body. Not all sugars, fats, and proteins have the same effect on the body. Sugars, fats, proteins found naturally in nature have been evolving with us for as long as we've been here. The sugars, fats, proteins from plants, like fruits and vegetables, do not have the same damaging effects that man-made or man-altered sugars, fats, and proteins have because we have been evolving along with them for millions of years. Our bodies know them and are very comfortable with those plant-derived molecules that we have formed deep, complex chemical relationships with over the last few million years.

Sugars, fats, and proteins found in nature are found in complex relationships with other molecules. They work together as a system. They have been working as an intimate system for way longer than our species has been here. Natural sugars, fats, and proteins have been evolving with all of their associated parts for billions of years, as well as the relationships between all those parts. Our bodies know those relationships because that is how our cells exist. Our Human cells have been in intimate relationships with naturally occurring sugars, fats, and proteins for millions and millions of years. Our Human bodies have been programmed to work along with those billions-of-years-old molecules and everything deep inside of them.

*By the way, plants have the exact same sequence of genes in their DNA that we have in our DNA that allows us and them to break down sugars.*

The deep cellular energy vibrational waves from the sugars that we have been evolving with for millions of years enhances us and our bodies. They do not act the same as man-made sugars do. They work with us, not against us. Also, you cannot overeat natural sugars. They naturally give our brains a feeling of satiety (a feeling of being full), so we don't and can't overeat them. I tested this on myself. You should do the same if you like. I tried to eat as much modern man-made processed sugar (white bread) as I could then the next day tried to eat as much natural sugar (natural unprocessed honey) as I could. It wasn't even close. I got really full, really fast on the natural honey. Not so much on the white bread.

## A Deeper look into natural-acting molecules versus man-made/altered molecules:

*The sugars, fats, proteins, or any molecule or chemical for that matter, that can cause profound long-term damage and acute inflammation within us do not behave like the natural ones. First off, some of us Humans think we can alter something that has been in the making since the beginning of our planet and claim that it works better and is healthier for us. If the sugar molecule, or any molecule, has been around for billions of years and has developed unique dependable relationships with neighboring molecules, how does our species think that it could alter that and not cause any damage within us? If our species has developed a healthy life-enhancing relationship with any molecule or any subatomic vibrational pattern over a multi-million year time period, then that relationship would be much stronger than anything modern man could ever think of making at present time.*

*As with any molecule, not just sugar, comes unique relationships (think sodium and chlorine developing a relationship in the form of the highly usable salt). These relationships have been working out the kinks (wasted time or wasted energy) for billions of years. They haven't changed much during that time because they eventually figured out how to exist because they figured out how to be efficient. They stayed with what worked and spent millions of years mastering those relationships.*

*Then our species comes along. We spend millions of years evolving with those molecules (like naturally-occurring proteins, carbs, and fats) that have been themselves evolving and adapting. We become one with those molecules, all of them. We form high functioning and highly adaptable relationships with all of these molecules. For millions of years, our species has formed complex, intimate relationships with the natural molecules present in our environment. Our immune system, digestive system, all of our systems, including our brains have all developed under these long-established intimate relationships deep within our cells. So, in turn, any and all of the cells inside of us are heavily dependent on the relationships encountered by the types of the molecules that enter us. Whether we breathe or ingest these molecules, they must be processed. And in most realities, there are only three possible reactions. The molecules taken into our bodies can either:*

*1. enhance our own molecules*

*2. disrupt them or*

*3. have no effect*

We'll jump back into this in a few sections.


{3.11} So now that I had a pretty decent understanding of the basics of health and how I could intellectually avoid preventable deaths, I was ready to fine-tune my long-term exercise and diet plan.

I tackled exercising first. Now that I had a little more knowledge about our basic species health, I would build up from that. Even if I was going through an extended period of my life where I did not have the time to take care of my health like I wanted to, at least I knew a few basic principles that would keep me from falling too far away from average health. At least I knew to keep moving and eat more natural foods. That alone would help my health from falling too far.

Of course, I needed and wanted more than "just keep moving" as a lifelong exercise plan. I experimented with many types of exercises. I was open to anything. What I was looking for was becoming more and more focused. As I played out my life and pictured myself as a 90-year-old version of me, I asked myself if this type of exercise would be beneficial to myself then as it would now? Would it benefit me at any age? I needed something that did not cause long-term damage while having numerous long-lasting health benefits. I also did not want to spend a lot of time exercising.

For whatever reason, I kept coming back to gymnasts. I was fascinated with how their bodies became so strong and sculpted by rarely lifting any weight. Their bodies were in optimal human shape without much running or lifting weights. How was that possible? Becoming stronger and more fit without conventional exercises?

What separated the gymnast was a very simple and often overlooked concept. Holds. They were training their muscles. They were training their muscles to hold the position rather than just move it in repetition. Those holds were the key to many "under the radar" health benefits.

Lifting heavy weights or running for an extended period of time can cause damage to our bodies. So those were out as long-term options. But what if we dropped the amount of weight we were using and focused more on pauses and holds instead of the number of repetitions?

The lighter weights would not cause long-term damage. What about the benefits of this type of exercise? Once I went over the benefits of resistance training, it became clear that I needed to include it in my lifelong goals.

Resistance was the key to so many underlying health benefits. Not weight, not reps, or not how long I worked out. Whether it was resistance from my own body weight, rubber bands, or light weights, the benefits were plentiful and long-lasting at any age.

One of the keys to resistance training is the pulling on the bone by the muscle. When we consistently have resistance on our bones by our pulling muscles, it tells our brain that we need to build up that area. We need to build up the bone, especially where the muscle attaches to it. Our bodies are highly intelligent. It will not waste time, energy, and resources on areas we do not use. However, if there is a part of our body and brain that is used repeatedly and consistently, it's marked as important, and more resources are sent to that area.

When we train our body with resistance training accompanied with holds and pauses, the benefits are many. Here are some of the benefits:

1. The action of a muscle pulling on a bone tells the body it needs to respond. It needs to build up the bone to the point of handling

the pull from the muscle. Hence, stronger brain and nerve-muscle connection.

2. It takes energy to build bone and muscle. Sugar and other energy molecules can be taken from the blood. This naturally lowers sugar in the blood. Helps prevent blood diseases (like too much sugar in the blood).

3. Exchange of important minerals (like calcium and phosphorus) and vitamins, between our bones and our blood, are enhanced and become more easily accessible. A balance between all of these essential nutrients start to level out.

4. Helps to reduce anxiety. Increased muscle activity helps to diminish high levels of stress and anxiety. Because of the disastrous effects that mental stress has on the health of our cells, this is most likely the most beneficial benefit of this type of exercise.

5. It burns calories. It burns calories for nearly 40 hours after exercising this way, allowing our muscles to pull on our bones. In contrast, running only burns calories for 2-4 hours after we run. It takes a lot of energy to balance out blood levels, build bone, and build muscle fibers. That type of energy requirement lasts for a long time. Resistance training burns calories for almost two days (~40 hours) after the workout.

6. Helps to balance out several hormones throughout the body.

7. Builds and strengthens our muscles, which improves our posture as well as our looks.

8. Our bodies become healthier and stronger and better-looking overall.

Since the effects of this type of exercise lasted for several days, time spent exercising was drastically cut. If I did these types of exercises right, it would only last 20-30 minutes, 2-3 days per week. Less than two hours per week for all of these benefits. Not bad at all.

My strength gradually increased as well. My body posture improved. My confidence went up as well.

To start, let's look at something as overlooked as pushups. There is a difference between doing 30 reps with no pauses and holds versus 10 reps with pauses and holds. The short-term benefits are different as are the long-term benefits. Push-ups use our own body weight as resistance. But instead of doing rep after rep, I tried to pause and hold after 3-4 repetitions. I would hold and pause during the middle of the repetition, not at the beginning or the end. I would hold it until my muscles started shaking and couldn't hold it anymore (pain). It was important (now looking back) to let my muscles struggle with holding the repetition. That's where most growth occurred. I was putting my muscles on the edge of frustration, where they were not comfortable.

We can use this technique with any and all of our muscle groups. It took me some figuring out but once I felt comfortable with it, it became a simple, dependable method to go to in order to reset. The long-term health benefits were numerous. I had to practice and work on this new type of workout. I had to practice to get the right feel of the correct angles of my body positions to fully stress my muscles to the point of them getting stronger.

I would eventually start to change the positions of my holds and pauses. As for push-ups, some of my holds would be at the bottom quarter of the rep, some would be in the middle of the rep, while others would be at the top quarter of the rep.

This is also a really good type of workout for our backs. Supposedly 80% of our species will eventually have lower back pains. By doing consistent light resistance exercises on our backs, we would be able to minimize some of our species' chronic back problems.

{3.12} Now that I had a go-to exercise plan in place, I turned my focus to my diet. If I wanted to live into old age and still be active and healthy, my current diet had to be changed. I needed to separate from the pack so to speak. If I ate like most of the Western World there was almost no chance that I was going to stay healthy deep into old age. I had to use what worked and had continuous benefits, not what made me feel accepted by society. I didn't care anymore about what other people thought about me and my lifestyle.

*I wanted to maximize my time on this planet, not waste it worrying if my friends and family would accept me if I ate or acted a certain way.*

Could I figure out a realistic, sustainable lifelong diet for me that would be able to enhance my life without taking too much of my time? Like exercising, I wanted a lot of "bang for my buck." 20-30 minutes of doing something that results in nearly 40 hours of benefits. I'll take that any day. I don't mind letting the body do what it's good at; building, repairing, and working. I wanted to find foods that would continually correct my potential health problems before they would get out of control. I needed high quality foods that enhanced the performance of my cells and me while performing high quality maintenance. I wanted to find foods that performed many "behind the scenes" functions. They would be providing a majority of the essential supplies and resources that would allow my cells to keep me performing at high levels.

So once again, I went back to the beginning. The beginning of us. Has our diet changed much since then? Are there clues in our history that I can use to figure out a diet that works for my lifestyle? Is there a diet that taps into the strength of our millions year old immune system? Is there a diet for us that takes away the stress of worrying about contracting a disease or succumbing to a lengthy illness? Something that builds me up and enhances my lifestyle without completely disrupting it?

For most of my life I despised and hated anything "natural." I hated natural foods, natural medicine, natural gardening, natural anything. I definitely did not believe eating had anything to do with my health. My family was introduced to natural foods when I was younger by my mom. She tended a garden and believed in eating healthy. The rest of my family, including me, mocked and looked down on her for thinking that way. I wanted to eat what I wanted, when I wanted. No greens for me, no salads, very few fruits and vegetables. "I only get one chance at this life," I would tell myself. "Why not live life to the fullest and not worry about food?

I have zero problems with me or anybody else having that kind of attitude. We all have the right to choose what we put in our bodies and no one else has the right to tell us what to put in our bodies. It's a waste of time anyway, worrying and stressing over someone else's diet, or lifestyle, for that matter. *We all need to be allowed to succumb to the long-term effects of our own choices, good or bad.*

But for me personally, my current diet was not matching up with my new life goals. If I wanted to live to 95-100 years old and still be active and healthy, something in my diet had to change. I wasn't even midway through my life, and I was starting to show signs of old age. Chronically inflamed joints, unwanted and unsightly body fat, digestion problems, low energy, high blood pressure, high cholesterol, etc., etc., etc. There was no way I was going to get close to a healthy old age going in this direction.

{3.13} So I had to discard my previous thoughts and beliefs I had about natural things. I had to pretty much dump most of my old thoughts and beliefs on everything. A total unbiased, stripped-down approach. No more bullshit excuses. Find out what works the best with the least amount of long-term harm, was my thinking. The answers that I needed may be in the places I have always refused to look.

I had to broaden my scope of how I looked at our species' diet. I had to take in the entirety of it. Nearly the entire existence of our species, over millions and millions of years, we've been eating what's readily available to us. Our entire digestive system, along with our life-dependent partners (the all-important Gut Bacteria), have been developing, adapting, evolving along with what was available in nature, naturally occurring, untouched and not manipulated by man.

For millions and millions of years, we lived in and among the natural world. Then everything started to change in the middle of the 1900s (1940, 50s, and 60s). Modern man enters the picture. He, along with his species-debilitating arrogance and ignorance, thinks he can make a food that's superior to what we've evolved and adapted with and to for millions of years. Even agriculture over the last 10,000 years was still pretty close to its natural state. Modern man did not molest or have a chance to manipulate its natural state...yet.

The evidence to me was becoming quite clear. Any individual, family, city, culture, or country that dominated their diet with modern foods far removed from their natural state would have the same pattern of diseases show up. Chronic inflammation, chronic pain, obesity, diabetes, heart attacks, strokes, cancer, etc., etc., etc. Even diseases like ADHD and Alzheimers would continually show up in these diets that were far removed from their natural state. Even psychological diseases would start to show up at a greater rate. There is a boatload of information out there staring us in the face telling us how unhealthy modern man-made foods are. My life on this planet could be shortened by decades because of these "modern" foods.

I knew I had to eat differently than others to live to an old age. I had to figure out what foods were close to their natural state and develop a lifelong plan to get more of them inside of me. I also had to build enough confidence to be able to eat differently while withstanding any possible attacks and intense judgments from others.

That turned out to be a much bigger challenge than I thought. I didn't realize what I ate would cause so much tension with other people. I was ridiculed, mocked, isolated, and looked down on. For what? For cleaning up *my own diet* that had nothing to do with them! It made me realize that worrying about what anybody does to their own bodies was pointless and a huge waste of my time and energy. I had a faint feeling that continually came up that I was unsure about until a few people voiced this, "Do you think you are better than me because you eat healthy?" This is when I realized it wasn't about the food I was eating. It was about them feeling threatened. Because when I looked back to how I used to feel about people eating healthy when I was against it, I was the same. I felt threatened. I mocked them, ridiculed them, and looked down upon them. I got what I deserved. However, the underlying theme was not about the food, but about how we quickly judge each other when we are insecure and feel threatened in any way.

I could not be that type of Human anymore. I fell into so many of our species' pitfalls over and over again. No more! I had to out-think our species' continuous problems.

As I look back to when I was a close-minded, judgmental Human, I question the reason why. Why was I so insecure when other people around me said or did something that was different than what I believed? Why did I feel the overwhelming need to be constantly accepted? Because even as dumb as I was when I was younger, I knew somewhere deep within me that healthy foods would probably be good for me in the long run. But of course, eating fruits and vegetables would make me seem less-than and unpopular, so I chose not to eat healthy. For two decades I chose being accepted by others and being thought of as "cool" over taking care of the health of my own body.

And it started to show. Unsightly belly fat, chronic inflammation in my joints, high blood pressure, high cholesterol, low energy, congested liver, and continual digestive problems. As I looked around at our species and compared my habits with others, it wasn't hard to find that those of us who ate unhealthily were all on similar paths. Paths to early death and chronic health problems.

I had to figure out a way to rise above the pull other people had on me. Changing my diet as well as my mindset regarding my diet was hard enough. But the real challenge was escaping the all-powerful, ever-present bad influence others had on my decision making. That was completely my problem, not theirs. I was weak...

I again went heavy on "behind the scenes" work. While my confidence wasn't strong enough early on to withstand the onslaught of disapproval, I changed and worked on what I needed to work on away from everyone. I worked on my faults, my health, my skills, everything without anyone knowing what I was doing. I couldn't stand the constant, unnecessary pressure other people would put on me. So, I slowly worked on myself without anyone knowing anything. I would do that until I built up enough inner confidence and self-worth to be me in front of others and be able to withstand the pressure.

*As crazy as this is going to sound, I will say it anyway. I thought about serial killers at this point in my adventure. Some serial killers lived completely normal lives in public. Many people around them liked them and hung out with them all while they were killing people "behind the scenes." If serial killers could have normal lives while performing*

*horrendous acts with no one knowing anything, I thought that I should
be able to build up a high level of self-worth and confidence "behind the
scenes" as well, with nobody knowing anything. And I didn't have to kill
anybody to do it!*

{3.14} Back to food. What were foods close to their "natural state"?
What have we been eating for the last few million years? What were we
eating for 99.999% of our existence?

Definitely not what was currently in my diet. My brain again went
deep; to where the life force of living things are found. I started with
the obvious foods we were probably eating much of. Plants. I'm pretty
sure most of our diet was composed of a high percentage of plant foods
(vegetables, fruits, herbs, nuts, grains) with a lower percentage of wild
animal meat. Plants could not run away from us, so therefore it's safe
to assume we ate more plants than animals for 99.999% of our species'
existence.

Then I hit another hurdle, eating fruits and veggies was messing
with my mind. I was brought up in an environment that were primarily meat eaters who looked down on those who ate fruits and
veggies. So, I not only had to build enough confidence to withstand
the pressure from others, I had to break away from my own thoughts
and beliefs about eating more plants. I looked for evidence to show
my toxic, stupid mind how idiotic that kind of thinking was. I found
what I was looking for in nature. Gorillas. How could anybody look
down on gorillas? They have incredible strength coupled with unwavering confidence. A 300 pound male gorilla is no joke. Incredible
strength, unwavering confidence, exceptionally high intelligence. A
total badass! Their diet? 99% plants! A large male gorilla can and does
eat up to 80 pounds of fruits and vegetables every day. Very little meat.

Were the adults around me—who I trusted to give me good, helpful information—wrong about despising fruits and veggies? Oh Yeah! They were way off. But to their credit, most of our species have no idea how to eat. I sure did not know how to eat. They and I were just following what everyone else would say or do without questioning anything. However, this is one of the many reasons I stopped listening to the advice from many of the adults throughout our species. The vast majority of the adults of our species (educated and uneducated) give terrible advice. It's mostly one-sided advice that usually leans toward them benefitting somehow.

***If adult Humans were wrong about something so important, could they be wrong about other basic fundamentals of our species?***

If a plant-dominated diet benefitted a gorilla, would it do the same for me? I had to find out. It did not take much searching. There is plenty of evidence showing a plant-dominant diet benefits us in countless ways. Top athletes got even better after switching to a plant-dominated diet. Stronger, healthier, quicker, just like the gorilla.

But in reality, I thought a 90-99% plant-dominant diet was too restrictive for me. Plants in my diet were the absolute key for me to live a long healthy life but I needed more flexibility, more adaptability.

And if I was going to include more plants in my diet, I wanted the ones that would offer the greatest benefits. I did not want to waste time and money on fruits and veggies that had little effect on my long-term health, because the health of any plant determines the overall effect it has on our bodies. Healthier plants make healthier food. Healthier food makes a healthier, stronger body. I wanted the best plants I could get into my body. The healthiest plants come from the healthiest soils. Soils, and the diversity of life within them, are the foundations of a healthy plant. Healthy plants taste better, resist disease better, fight off pests better, and provide a large amount of easy-to-use, life-energizing, life-enhancing nutrients.

Same as everything else in life, diversity was key. The soils that had a lot of life (bacteria, fungus, insects, earthworms) in them were always better at producing healthier plants. Soils that had little to no life in them produced less healthy plants. These plants had little taste, very few usable nutrients, were more susceptible to disease and pest, and surely did not offer the same amount of energy that the healthier soil produced. I could also taste the difference in each bite.

So just eating any ol' fruit or veggie wasn't going to cut it. However I got them, the majority of the fruits and veggies I ate needed to come from life-enhancing, naturally nutrient-dense soil.

What were fruits and veggies anyway? What were they made of?

Plants have organs just like you and me. Our liver is an organ. Our lungs are organs. Organs are made up of highly important living cells. The root of a plant is an organ. The leaves on a plant are their organs. Plant cells like our human cells are made up of molecules like proteins, carbohydrates, and fats. Those molecules are made up of atoms (like sodium and chlorine making salt). Atoms are made up of subatomic particles (protons, neutrons, electrons). Those subatomic particles are driven and controlled by **ENERGY** and any energy waves that come off of them. ((think of waves (ripples)) of water coming off of a rock that was thrown into water)).

There is an energy between these subatomic particles. It drives everything. This is the driver of all living things. It controls the performance of everything above it, from the cells to the tissues, to the organs, to us. The overall effect it has on our entire body, good or bad, may take decades to express itself. It takes a lot of time for altered energy waves deep within our atoms to eventually express as a disease in our organs that we notice. I ate poorly and neglected my personal health for many years before I started to notice the damage. Nearly two decades of a poor diet before I fell into the typical health problems; chronic pain, high blood pressure, high cholesterol, low energy, etc.

In its natural state, the energy found deep inside the fruit or veggies' cells is life-enhancing. This energy can energize and give life to the atoms, molecules, cells, tissues, organs, and the entire plant. The vibrational wave energy that is given off of these naturally occurring subatomic particles is strong and consistent. It allows all above it to perform at a much higher level. The plant performs better and in turn, those true, natural, strong, consistent life-enhancing vibrational waves that were deep in those plants can be transferred to us. After we eat and breakdown and absorb those types of plants, that highly productive natural energy influences the wave patterns deep within *our* subatomic particles. They influence them in a very positive way. They lift their energy to highly productive levels. Then that newly energized energy is passed to the molecules, then to the cells, then to the organs, and then eventually to us.

At this point I really felt if I increased the percentage of plants in their most natural state, it would slowly but surely improve everything inside of me.

If plants evolved with us for the last few million years it would seem that they had a lot to do with our overall health and existence. It would make sense that many of our human functions, or at least top level functioning, revolved around our relationship with plants.

It is also safe to assume (*although I usually don't like assuming, but sometimes it can work*) that when we alter our food, plants or meats, from its natural state, we alter the energy found deep within them.

Once we alter that vibrational energy that has evolved with us for so long, we alter how everything functions above that. Erratic, inconsistent, or weak energy waves in an atom controls molecules, cells, tissues, organs and eventually us. Grab a handful of rocks and throw them into a pool of water and watch the ripples (waves). Random waves are colliding with other random waves in a very inconsistent flow. It would be hard to imagine anything getting much useful energy from that mess. Too much inconsistent chaos.

This is possible to me and you deep within us when we continually, for long periods of time, introduce stuff into our bodies that change or inhibit the true life-giving natural energy. Plants, chemicals, meats, water, the air we breathe, etc. Anything that enters our bodies must be processed. Anything that enters our body can have an effect on our body, noticeable or not noticeable...

*There are only three effects that can happen when something enters our minds, brains, and body.*
*1. They can have a positive effect and enhance performance.*
*2. They can have a negative effect and disrupt, causing harm.*
*3. They can have a neutral, no effect at all.*

{3.15} What alters that energy deep within our cells? Anything that enters our minds, our brain, our eyes, our noses, our mouth, our skin, can have an effect on the vibrational energy given off by our cells. Our cells have a memory. Their memories are stored as vibrations deep within their atoms. Think about something that triggers a painful memory from your past, something that hurts. If it triggers a painful memory, your body and brain will respond defensively. Our mind and brain will try to keep us from going there again because it signals danger. The vibrations deep within our cells change and are remembered.

If those vibrations are felt again, our fight or flight response system may kick in. It is a much-needed type of defense we benefit from. However, these dangerous, trauma vibrations can disrupt normal cell functions.

When I thought deeply about my greatest fears, something physical would change. My mind, brain, and body did not want to go near those fears. There was something so painful that my body and mind was trying to keep me from going there. Sometimes when I got too close to those deep feelings of that fear deep within me, I would start shaking and sweating profusely.

If just thinking about my fears would cause a physical reaction deep within my cells, then I'm guessing that other things that entered my body would cause reactions as well. So, starting with my diet was much easier for me than working on my deep fears...at least, at this point. But I knew when I gained more inner strength and confidence, I was going back to face those fears. I had to. They were the controlling forces over most of my decision making. I had to find out what decisions I would be making if I overcame those fears. I had one or two core fears, but I also had several smaller, yet still disruptive fears that I needed to overcome as well. I wanted and needed to see what I was to become if I faced and defeated those fears that have controlled me for so long.

### Video Game Analogy:

*This new, challenging, scary, yet exciting adventure I was on really felt like I was in a video game. I started off in the lower easier levels with very few usable skills, tools, or much knowledge of where I was going. Slowly but surely, I built up my skills, tools, and knowledge a little at a time. And at the end of each "level" it seemed that I usually had to "defeat" an enemy. The "end of level enemy" was either a person in my life trying to keep me down or it was my own internal fears and self-doubt that were also holding me down.*

*Nearly every time I learned something new or made myself a little better, there was somebody right there to question what I was doing and to ridicule and mock it as to defeat me. And many times, just like in the video game, I lost to that "end of the level enemy," where I did not have the knowledge or confidence to stand up to them. I would lose. They would win.*

*However, just like in video games, those types of people have very predictable moves. And once you play against them a few times with an open mind, you quickly pick up on their weaknesses and their patterned attacks. And by then you've gained a little more knowledge and a few more usable skills and tools. Once you "defeat" them, you can move on to the next "level."*

*Some of my lower level "enemies" I had to "defeat" or stand up to were my friends. I had to be my true self around them no matter if they accepted me or not, or whether they tried to hold me back. I did not want to follow their lead, but I was too weak to say no.*

*Some of the higher level "end bosses" that I would eventually have to face and defeat were family and relationship inequality issues. I had to become more equal in my relationships, either if I was above them or below them, they needed to be equalized. I either needed to lower and humble myself to equal myself to the people who I thought were lower than me, or I had to pick myself up to the level of the people who thought they were greater than me. My boss (or job) was another "enemy" I needed to rise up against. Since I had no other job skills other than the job skills I needed for the job I had, I was stuck. If I was stuck, it meant I was dependent on someone else for my income. If I was dependent on someone else for my income, I was naturally lower than them.*

*Once I "learned the game" and built a lot of different skills and abilities, I was no longer lower than my boss. I exceeded their control over me. I no longer needed just that one job. I could "defeat" them and move on to other "levels" or careers. The same was true for every single thing I have ever tried to overcome.* **To get to the point where I was in control of my game, not the game controlling me!**

*So just like in video games, I had to build my skills and knowledge in the lower levels (defeat my basic, more simpler problems) to be able to eventually face my deeper, darker, more challenging problems. In the first few "levels," I lacked confidence, knowledge, and skills. But with each level of completion, I gained a little more confidence, knowledge, and skills. If I would have faced my deepest, darkest problems in the first level, I would have been destroyed rather quickly.*

{3.16} Back to our species' diet. I knew I was going to have to increase the percentage of plants in my eating habits while also increasing the amount of all types of foods closest to their natural state. If I ate more foods closer to their natural state, I would most likely *not* have to give up any foods, good or bad. Is it possible to live a long healthy life while not giving up our favorite foods?

That's where percentages came in. It was helpful to figure out a comfortable percentage that would not be too restrictive but also healthy. I needed and wanted freedom, but I also wanted to live a long healthy life.

I experimented with various percentages. Each diet I was on lasted for several years. Diets lasting for only a few months don't really do much of anything. That's not long enough to even give a chance for our gut bacteria to adapt and change to the new food. That itself takes 8-12 months. So, any diet that I wanted to try and learn and test on myself, I had to be on it for several years to truly feel the differences between them.

### *Diet 1*:
90% *Unnatural* modern processed foods with 10% foods in their *natural* state

### *Diet 2*:
10% *Unnatural* modern processed foods with 90% foods in their *natural* state

### *Diet 3*:
25% *Unnatural* modern processed foods with 75% Foods in their *natural* state

There is a strategy to this, and I learned this the hard way. With every new diet came a transition period. The transition period allowed my Gut Bacteria to adapt to my new diet. This would usually take 8-12 months. It was painful sometimes at the beginning with the digestive issues, if you know what I mean. However, the pain was minimized if I eased more slowly into the new diet. It took a little patience. The Turtle Approach!

We should not underestimate the power and importance of our gut bacteria. They have so much to do with our overall way of life. Treat them right and you and your body, brain, and mind will be rewarded. If we treat them wrong, we may pay some life-altering consequences. Our gut bacteria are talking with our brain constantly. There is a reason many call our gut bacteria our second brain. Their environment in our lower intestines is of the utmost importance and should not be altered much. Our species' gut bacteria have been evolving with us for millions of years. We have a very special relationship with them.

In the end, it was clear to me which diet worked the best for my long-term goals. I felt incredible during the 90% natural foods and 10% unnatural food diet. I had so much more energy. I felt and looked a decade younger than I was. Also, I never gave up any foods, just changed percentages around. I had a 10% pressure-release valve in place with this particular diet. I did not have to be perfect to achieve high-level results. Actually, trying to be 100% perfect was counterproductive in the long run. Too much pressure. Not much in life works well under constant high pressure. We don't either.

In all honesty, it took several years to show the most impressive results. If I would have stopped in year three, I never would have seen the benefits I would eventually get in year six. However, within the first year of the 90% natural and 10% unnatural diet, I was already starting to see chronic pain and inflammation disappear. I could kneel for several minutes when only 11 months earlier, I could only last for 3-5 seconds before my burning knee pain would cause me to stand up.

My digestion also started to improve within the first year. My allergies were also decreasing in frequency and intensity. Over the next few years, slowly but surely, many physical things started to improve. My energy levels increased, I slept better, halitosis (bad breath) decreased, and my blood pressure and cholesterol started to drop. But it was what happened to my immune system in years four and five that really opened my eyes to the power of eating high quality foods in their natural state. As it takes a while to cause long-term damage, it takes a while to reverse it and improve it. Patience and a long-term vision were essential for this. Turtle baby!

As the years went by, my immune system gained strength. I was getting sick much less. At one point, I went three years without any sickness, not even a cold. And when I did get sick, I would usually recover within 48 hours. There was no doubt anymore, the dietary changes I made years ago were starting to show. Even as I aged, my recovery time was quicker. Even with injuries like cuts, sprains, and pulled muscles, there was a much faster recovery time. There was one time that I severely pulled my lower back. Pinched a nerve while pulling a muscle. I could barely move for the next 24 hours. But 24 hours later, I was walking around. Another 24 hours after that, I was back to work. No Doctors. Treated and helped myself using very basic healing methods. Common sense goes a long way.

I remember how I used to be. I would get sick multiple times a year. Some illnesses would last for weeks. I've pulled back muscles before, less severely, and couldn't do much of anything for over a week. I was shocked and amazed at what a healthy human mind, brain, and body could do. And this was just the beginning.

We may not be able to stop the aging process, but we sure can slow it down. Matching high, pure, life-giving energy within us with similar types of energy from the environment around us will no doubt lift us to higher levels of life. If we *consistently* take in life-enhancing energy from the environment around us, that energy will infiltrate every part of us. That life-enhancing energy has been evolving within us for millions of years. Any extended time *away* from that kind of energy will cause problems within us. Any extended time *with* that type of energy will produce countless benefits.

Any of us can achieve this without giving up our favorite foods. I do not like being told what to do, so a restrictive diet telling me what to eat and what not to eat wasn't going to work for me, unless of course my body or a doctor was telling me that I needed to avoid certain foods for certain health reasons. Some foods, even natural foods, can have negative effects on our bodies if our bodies cannot handle them (whether a genetic problem or not), so experiment wisely.

I also did not want to be controlled by food. So, a highly flexible, adaptable diet was essential. As long as I ate natural foods more often than unnatural foods, I could maintain some decent level of health all on my own.

{3.17} Looking at a plate of food divided into percentages helped me get started. If three quarters of a plate was filled with natural, unprocessed food, I knew 75% of my meal was on the natural life-enhancing side. If half of the last quarter of my plate was covered in natural foods, then I knew I was close to 90%. That would take me three seconds. That last 10% was wide open. It could be anything I wanted. The sugariest, the fattest, the unhealthiest, it did not matter, the last 10% was a free-for-all. It was my pressure release from an all-restrictive diet. If I was on the 75% natural and 25% unnatural diet, then 25% of each plate was whatever I wanted that wasn't natural. The 75% natural and 25% unnatural diet offered me flexibility when I was going through those down times in my life and wasn't able to be on the 90% natural and 10% unnatural diet. It also kept my overall health from taking a huge dive. I did not have as much energy or the quick recovery time like the 90/10 natural/unnatural diet, but it was still pretty good. I believe most of us could avoid many common preventable diseases with this 75/25 diet, because we definitely would be able to on the 90/10 diet.

*Our performance as a Human depends on many things, and one of those things at the top of the list is the quality and the usability of the energy we intake...*

I will never underestimate the power of plants again.

--> For natural foods, I stuck to a wide variety of seasonal raw fruits and veggies along with cooked veggies. Wild meats, herbs, and nuts, were all increased in percentages. Natural eggs from chickens that were also on a 90% natural and 10% unnatural diet were also heavily eaten.

--> Animal meats and other non-plant products are also many times healthier closer to their millions year-old natural state.

Any individual or family that is in a constant struggle to get ahead in life, this is a great place to start and master. The underlying benefits of eating more foods in their natural state cannot be underestimated. They improve every aspect of our entire being, it improves our entire family infrastructure from the ground up going unnoticed. Of course, it cannot solve all problems, but it can help to minimize others that may show up, like behavior.

A child's behavior and mental ability has something to do with their food. Maybe not all of it, but I don't underestimate the power of food when it comes to behavior anymore. Anything that goes into our bodies, minds, or brains can have an influence on what comes out of our bodies, minds, or brains.

To me, it's a little like this: After I lost my career, I became pretty poor. I had trouble paying bills, had trouble paying everything. So, when I went to put food into my body, I had a thought. I was naturally going to put the cheapest food in it because I didn't have enough for much of anything. I had to get the cheapest food, right? Then I started thinking, what would be the long-term differences in the performance of my brain, body, and mind if I used cheaper, lower quality food versus the higher quality food? If I can't afford much right now, shouldn't I try to prevent some major expensive damage down the road. If I use the cheaper food, the lower quality of it may corrode my brain, mind, and body faster, causing more expensive problems later. If I would pay a little more money now and get higher quality food, it would help to prevent major damage later on. Even when I was at my lowest points, my poorest points in life, I still chose to spend a little extra money on higher quality food. The long-term benefits are too many, from spending less time and money on doctors and medications to having more energy to do...to be! Always thinking of those long-term effects...

{3.18} Now I had a solid plan. I was building something all my own. I was building a dynamic empire of self-derived confidence along with a host of lifelong skills and knowledge. I was becoming diversified. I was taking care of myself. I was taking care of my own life. I was becoming less and less dependent on others. The more skills I built, the more confidence I had. The more confidence I acquired, the easier life got. I wasn't wasting time and energy on things and people who wasted my time and energy.

I couldn't wait to see what my life would become. I never took these paths before. Every day was a new adventure, a new experience. And the best was yet to come.

As the years went by, that's how life played out. A new exciting life was unfolding before me, and I built it myself. Every year my skills expanded and got better. My intelligence was growing. My understanding of how things worked started becoming clearer. Slowly, year by year, changes deep within me were growing. I wanted more. I wanted to have more of these high-level experiences. I wanted that feeling with as many things that I could possibly have it with. I wanted to learn about as many different areas of life that I could.

I'm not sure why our species settled on teaching all of us that learning a few skills or jobs is the right way to go. It's not. To be free is to be able to do many things for yourself. That's my personal freedom.

I thought that was odd about us. Why aren't more of us really good and knowledgeable at many areas of life? Why are so many of us good or knowledgable at only one or two things?

It doesn't have to be that way for you and me. That's a decision that we all make for ourselves. There is zero evidence out there that points to the idea that we, as a species, are incapable of being really good and dominant at a wide variety of skills and abilities. All of us are highly capable of being a Dominant Human Being in many, many, many areas of our own lives while on this planet.

"Even if we could be really good at many different things throughout the course of our lives, how would I ever have the time to do it?" I asked myself nine years ago. "Is it even possible? It takes thousands of hours to become really good at just one thing." How would anybody have enough time to live a normal life with all of its required obligations while learning and mastering a variety of different skills, abilities, and intelligences?

That's what we figure out in the next chapter...We'll also try to figure out which Human personality trait would be the most influential trait to work on first. Which trait could we work on first that would have the most effect on other traits? With time, could we improve one trait to the level that it would start to enhance and improve other traits within our personalities?

# Chapter 4

# Finding Time to Find Me

{**4.1**} How and when do I find the time to build a better me? It can quickly become overwhelming when trying to figure out how to rebuild ourselves, along with the rest of life's regular activities. How can I rebuild my inner self, my intelligence, my confidence, while building up a vast array of skills while maintaining a normal life? "Is there even enough time to do this?" I asked myself.

First off, we all have the same 24 hours in a day. Some of us can accomplish a wide variety of things within that same 24-hour period. All of the "Greatest," most accomplished Humans that have ever lived, all had the same 24 hours a day you and I have. All of the greatest Human accomplishments were carried out by people with the same 24-hour days we all have. If they can do it, so can we. We also realize now that being the greatest and the best at anything puts too much unnecessary pressure on ourselves, making our lives harder and less fun. I personally settled on being pretty good at as many things that I could possibly be versus great or the best at one or two things.

Diversity and balance are two of the driving forces for a meaningful, independent free life.

When I put most of my time and energy into being something great in only one or two areas of my life, all the other areas suffered greatly. My diversity of life dropped, my balance became unbalanced, and I lost most of my freedom. Then I became too dependent on others for those neglected areas of my life.

*I wanted and needed more personal freedom. I was beginning to realize the more dependent I was on other people, the less freedom I had. Therefore, the less skills I had to fall back on, the more dependent I was on others, and the less freedom I had. I had to learn more and keep learning.*

{4.2} I, like most of us, had a full life; career, family obligations, social life, hobbies, travel, etc. How was I going to find the time to build my inner confidence while building a variety of skills and knowledge that would make me less dependent on others?

I started by breaking down, by minutes and hours, how much time I spent doing various activities. I crudely broke them down to productive time versus unproductive time. I also broke down an average day and week worth of hours to visually see how my days were broken down. This would help me to see where and how many wasted hours there were. If I could swap out some of those unproductive hours with productive hours without interfering with my current life, it may work. It would take some time, but eventually, by working on several things at a time for short periods of time I could become good at a wide variety of things in my life.

## *Example 1: Weekdays only*

*+24 hours*

- *7 hours for sleeping*
- *8 hours for work*
- *3 hours for eating*
- *1 hour for self-maintenance/cleaning*

*= +5 hours left per day (which could be divided to spend quality time with our kids and then also quality time with ourselves)*

*= +25 hours left per week (not including the two day weekend)*

*= +41 hours left per week (including weekends) (+ ~16 hours for Saturday and Sunday)*

*=+ 100 hours left per month (not including the two day weekends)*

*= +164 hours left per month (including weekends)*

## *Example 2: Weekdays only*

+24 hours

- 8 hours for sleeping
- 10 hours for work
- 3 hours for eating
- 1 hour for self-maintenance/cleaning

= +2 hours left per day (could split between kids and yourself or entirely for our kids)

= +10 hours left per week (not including weekends)

= +30 hours left per week (including weekends)

= +40 hours left per month (not including weekends)

= +120 hours left per month (including weekends)

*** If we have kids, ½ to ¾ of our free time should probably be spent with them. The benefits from consistent parental quality time with our kids is unmeasurable. The long-term benefits are huge and should never be* *underestimated. The younger they are, the higher percentage of our free time should be given to them. As they grow and become less dependent on us, more of our free time will come back to us. More on this in Chapter 6.*

Once I saw the breakdown, I couldn't believe how many extra hours I had during the week. Why did I have so few skills? What was I doing with those extra hours? Even if I chilled and relaxed for an hour or a few hours, I still had plenty of time left over to build myself into something worthwhile. If I balanced out my unproductive time with a little more productive time, then I could do it. I could slowly, patiently, and at my own comfortable pace, rebuild my life and my personality. I had a very strong force driving me to find something better. The drive to become dependent on myself, no more on others. No more depending on others for my needs. I knew I needed to build a better, smarter brain. I knew I needed a wide variety of skills and knowledge to become less dependent on others. One of my biggest obstacles from the beginning was finding the time. I found some holes in that obstacle.

{4.3} I began to break down the extra hours I had. I broke down productive time versus unproductive time. I even broke down unproductive time and productive time during work hours. Was there unproductive time during work hours that I could use to build me while not interfering with work? I soon realized at any job, no matter how small or insignificant it may seem, you can build a very powerful brain. It just involved a tweak or two in my perception. As usual, and forever always, our perception on anything makes us or breaks us. And we have full control of our perception.

*I began to see any job as a new skill builder. Every new skill I built, the closer I was to my personal freedom. No longer would I have to stay in a job working for an abusive, unintellectual boss. I would no longer be stuck in one place if I had a wide variety of skills to take me to other places. It put the power and control on my side.*

But, as with most worthwhile things in life, it was quite challenging. It was very challenging dealing with my self-perceived image; to humble myself into taking jobs that were well beneath my worth and my previous success. I previously had a long successful career before deciding to leave to become more independent. It was an epic internal battle inside me to lower myself that much. I went from making nearly $80,000 down to $13,000 a year during a very low 3-year period. The financial pressure was complete torture. But I never gave up on myself. I never gave up on my plan for long-term success. I never gave up on my brain and my mind sitting in my head. I now knew what it was capable of. And while I was financially poorer than I've ever been in my adult life, I built more skills than the entirety of the rest of my life during those three years. I was tired of being a punching bag in life. I was tired of everyone telling me what to do and who to be. I was also tired of making too many decisions based on money. I was tired of the pressure I felt from the people around me.

So, I gave up making decisions based on money or what others thought of me. After my lost career, I could basically only work in just two fields. After I tossed out my pride and focused on building me, I began to work in areas I knew little about. Those three years I spent doing those different, supposedly meaningless low paying jobs, produced more worthiness and more skills than all the higher salary jobs I previously had. After three years, I was capable of working in 10 different fields. I was no longer dependent on one or two types of jobs. I was getting a little closer to my own personal freedom!

{**4.4**} I had another recurring thought that would help me restart my ambitions and goals and keep my long-term plans going. It would also help me from falling too deep back into the unbalanced, unproductive time for too long.

*What would I think of my life and what I did with it when I think back over it when I'm in my 70s, 80s, 90s? Would I be happy with how I spent my time here? Would I be happy and content with my life decisions I made? Was I okay with being so dependent on others for the quality of my life? Would I be okay with never exploring the deep, most fascinating areas of my own brain and mind? Would I be okay with only learning a few things while I'm here?*

In short, hell no, I wasn't going to be content with that. I felt there was enough evidence around me and in me to reliably predict how my life was going to turn out if I didn't change course. If I didn't take time to build myself, to build a better me, all I had to do was look at how I lived for the majority of my life. Every relationship had the same outcome, every job had the same outcome. I was dependent on those relationships just as I was dependent on those jobs with those paychecks. I was never really free and most of that was my own fault.

I had one chance at this life, I did not want to waste too many hours on things that did not enhance my life. I never really quit doing anything; I actually expanded the diversity of the entertainment I used to relax and reset, and just decreased the amount of time they owned my life. For example, I love movies and TV, so I wasn't about to give them up, but I also wasn't going to let them take over my life. My life became so much more than sitting in front of a screen watching somebody else live life. I felt the 90-year-old version of myself would be incredibly disappointed if I spent most of my extra time on unproductive hours of self-entertainment and self-gratification. No building of any skills or abilities, no exploration of our brain and mind, just hour after hour looking at a screen watching others.

My unproductive time, however, was not just found in the usual places like TV, phone, or internet. I found most of my unproductive, wasteful time deeply embedded in my social relationships with people around me in my everyday life. This type of unproductive time can and most likely will be more toxic than any unproductive time watching TV. TV and other forms of entertainment can be a very helpful way to relax and unwind from the stresses of life. It just caused me problems when it became a dominant part of my life, creating an imbalance. But wasted time dealing with people who think they are better than us is a bigger waste of time and energy. I didn't care if they were close family, close friends, co-workers, or anyone; if they thought that they were better than me as a Human and they treated me as an unequal less-than, my time spent with them was drastically reduced or eliminated. Either I completely cut them out of my life or spent very little time with them.

As we are a social species and we do thrive when we are around others, we can also suffer the consequences of putting too much emphasis on having relationships with someone who treats us as unequal. We are a square peg forced into a round hole kind of species. Just because mankind continually tells us that we should stay in certain relationships no matter what, it doesn't mean that is correct. Staying in any relationship with a person who thinks they are above us can drastically alter our life, and most of the time it is not good. The most important relationship we can have is with ourselves anyway. We become dominant and self-confident in our own lives when we develop healthy relationships with ourselves. Learning how to talk to myself was crucial. Learning how to tell myself "NO" was critically important. Telling myself that *not* everything I thought of was always right, was epic! I finally told myself how wrong I was with many of my thoughts and ideas.

So much of the power of our species occurs when we allow ourselves the proper amount of time to reflect on our lives and reevaluate the outcomes of the choices we have made while others are not around influencing our thoughts. As we are a social species, some of our greatest strengths are found in our individual brains.

*The better and more balanced the individual brain and mind operate, the better the parent, the better the kid, the better the adult, the better the family, the better the neighborhood, the better the species.*

{4.5} So with that, I had to reevaluate the time I was spending with other people. Family or not, was that relationship causing me wasted time and energy? Because if you have a toxic relationship with someone, you not only lose the time while being in their presence, you lose energy. That energy loss costs you more lost time after they are gone. It's a double whammy. Lost energy and lost time. TV and other forms of entertainment rarely have that effect. Toxic, selfish people do.

But the opposite is true. If I'm around someone with good energy, I feel like I've gained time. If I'm around somebody that treats me like their equal while not trying to tell me how to live my life, I become energized to do more. I gain a little pep-in-my-step.

Whether time is wasteful or not in a relationship with another person depends highly on the energy between you and that person. *I had to remind myself continuously that I could be the one in the relationship that was causing the drop in energy*. It usually takes a pattern of behavior. If you feel a loss of energy and time after being around someone 1 out of 10 times, that's normal and okay. If you feel a loss of energy and time eight or nine out of 10 times after being around someone, that's a pattern and that's a problem. That relationship, no matter what kind, may be a waste of time and energy.

Even if it's family whom you have to spend time with, we can drastically cut down the time we spend with that person while not completely cutting them out. They can still treat me however they want, but I do not have to put up with it. If somebody did not accept my lifestyle because they didn't agree with it, family or not, they were going to see a lot less of me. I was growing tired of spending my valuable time with people, family or not, who looked down on me as I was less than them.

Other wasteful things to spend our mind on began to leap into my head. Spending any amount of time and energy worrying or getting frustrated by how another person or group of people live their lives. I have never, and may never, add up all the lost, pointless, wasted hours I've spent being aggravated with people who were different from me or had different beliefs or ideas than me. I would waste way too many hours trying to convince people to see things my way. What a gigantic waste of my life. Gossip, drama, lying, cheating, thinking others are less than me, and talking about other people behind their back are all massive energy and time wasters. These are all wasteful ways for our species to spend its time on Earth.

Once I cut back on excessively lazy entertainment and the toxic, wasteful people around me, I started to see a clear path toward personal freedom along with the time I needed to pull it off.

{4.6} A few minutes here and there can really add up over time. Continuously working on things was and is the key. It's more important than many hours at a time, every now and then, especially when we don't have large blocks of time to work on things.

*Remember, we can always work on things in our brains even though they are not in front of us.*

Take music for example, I've talked to countless adults who played musical instruments as kids only to stop after high school. I often wondered what would happen if they kept playing, 5 to 10 minutes every few days or so, every month or so. They surely wouldn't have become great only playing that little bit of time, but their musical skills wouldn't have diminished to nearly nothing either. Even if I didn't have huge blocks of time to devote to any one thing, I could continuously work on many different things a few minutes at a time. I most likely wouldn't become great at any one thing but I could be good at many different things.

The deep connections built in our brains are made when we continuously do something, say something, think something, etc... If we make it important, the brain will too. If we continually do something that is read as important by our brain, it then starts to build a stronger neural network to accommodate this repetitive activity. More expansive, stronger connections are built. The more we do it, the stronger the connections are. If I play piano for six hours every two months versus 20 minutes every week, what would happen? Six hours versus two hours and 40 minutes over those two months. There aren't many things that would be tagged as important by our brains if it happened every two months. It's too far apart to be considered consistent. If it only comes around every few months, why waste time and energy building a strong neural network? The brain's energy and resources will be put toward repetitive, consistent behaviors, good or bad.

Although two hours and 40 minutes over a two-month period wouldn't make enough strong brain connections for us to be really good, there are still some subtle benefits incubating underneath the surface. First off, whatever skills you have, you retain. They may not get better, but they won't diminish. They will always be there waiting for us to come back when we have time to work on them. If we keep doing something every week, even for a few minutes, our brains keep them relevant.

So now I figured out how much extra time I had each week along with the knowledge that I did not have to spend a large amount of my time trying to be good at many different things. That was immensely satisfying.

It's so important to learn at the pace you're comfortable with. Nobody has the right to tell us that we should put a certain time limit on our individual learning. At times I had to pull back my ambitions to make sure I wasn't just learning things on a surface, superficial level. This is where the role of practicing things in my mind came into play. I wanted to be free from the control of other people.

If I wanted to be truly free and independent, I needed to learn not only a wide variety of skills, I needed to learn them on a deeper level. So many of the people in our lives who try to control and manipulate us are surface, superficial learners/thinkers. They learn just enough to be able to be above us. They learn the right, big, fancy, smart-sounding words and meanings to gain advantages over us. They know the exact phrasing and tone of what they are telling us so we would think they know so much and are so great. I had to get past that level. I had to get to the level of knowledge that they cared not to go to, the deeper levels of learning.

We can all get to that deeper level of learning. We can all do it yet very few of us ever venture that deep. I would get to the deeper levels of understanding of how something works by exploring the places in our species' brain most of us avoid.

When I learned as a kid, I had no preconceived beliefs or ideologies to alter my decision making. When I stripped MY opinions away, learning became easier. My decisions as a kid were based on common sense, not opinions and self-derived beliefs. Learning new skills, or anything, as a kid, was so exciting. I wanted to go back to loving learning as I did as a kid.

{4.7} I developed a long list of things I wanted to learn, build, and accomplish. Each decade of my life became a new era to learn and create entirely new areas in my life. For the first decade I chose to intensely work on my personality. My low levels of confidence and self-worth was my number one priority from the beginning. Our personalities are very much like the soil that nourishes a garden or a forest. Especially confidence, since it's one of the main ingredients to a healthier us. The more diverse, healthy, and balanced the soils are, the stronger the garden and forest plants will be. The veggies in the garden as well as the plants in the forest are undeniably more resistant to attacks from bad stuff from virtually anything, when growing in soil that is diverse, healthy, and adaptable versus the opposite.

Same with our personalities; the more diverse, healthy, balanced, and adaptable our personalities are, the more adversity we can withstand. Since working on my entire personality was overwhelming, I chose to only work on one fault at a time. I thought long and hard on which one to work on first. Which trait could I work on from the beginning that would have the most profound trickling-up effect (the ability to influence many other parts of my personality)?

Self-built Inner Confidence! Self-built Inner Confidence! Self-built Inner Confidence!

*For the most part, I built up a wide variety of lifelong skills along with several ways to build my creative side of the brain without anybody knowing. Until my confidence was higher, I could not handle the pressure and judgment people put on me. I was going to build a better me the way I was comfortable with, away from people and their influence.*

I became a much happier person this way. It took so much pressure off of me. I gave myself very loose time frames to work on myself. I just knew I did not want to stop working on the gifts I had deep inside of me. We all have insanely, incredible gifts deep within us. We just have to dig them out. I was determined to find out what hidden gifts were waiting to be found. In what areas in this life might I actually be good at that I may have never tried before?

I made a promise to myself to work on the intense, darker parts of my mind and brain just as much as I worked on learning more about the things in my life that made me happy. If I was going to work on the hardest parts of my personality—my faults—I was also going to reward myself by doing more of what made me happy as well. Balance, baby!

And working on your personality consistently for a few minutes every few days can produce much needed momentum throughout. I did not have to spend an enormous amount of time working on myself either. Too much is exhausting anyway. I gave myself nearly unlimited time and nearly an unlimited amount of mistakes from the beginning of any new thing I was trying to learn. I just couldn't quit. If I quit, I would go back to the person I used to be. That was not going to happen.

**I gave myself a decade or so to develop a decent understanding of the following:**

1. Understanding and controlling my raw feelings and emotions.

2. Build up my own self-worth and self-derived inner confidence to higher, more sustainable levels.

3. Re-establish the love of learning I had as a kid.

4. Identify and diminish my personality flaws.

5. Learn more about areas of life that I dislike, hate, or don't understand.

6. Develop a variety of basic, fundamental cooking skills.

7. Learn how to grow my own food.

8. Understand the relationship between my food and my health.

9. Learn how different ecosystems work on deep levels.

10. Learn how to enhance, maintain, and nurture the nature and outdoors that I use for recreation.

11. Learn how not to get lost by building a sense of direction.

12. Start building the creative parts of my brain (arts, music, etc.) as well as the unused parts of my brain.

13. Develop a variety of basic medical skills to be able to treat myself for basic health issues.

14. Observe, open-mindedly and unbiasedly, the behavioral similarities between animals, children, and adults.

15. Learn how houses are built and how they work.

16. Learn basic carpentry, electrical, and plumbing skills to be able to repair and build.

17. Learn, at least to a comfortable, decent level, two musical instruments.

18. Figure out a good go-to type of exercise.

19. Figure out a common sense, lifelong enhancing diet.

20. Learn basic mechanic skills. Small engine and some basic automobile.

21. Learn how to dominate and minimize daily chores.

22. Learn, unbiasedly and open-mindedly, how the planet and the universe works, at least on a basic level.

{4.8} As I'm writing this book nine years after making this list, I can now look back to see where I stand. As daunting as that list is as I just wrote it out, I'm quite pleased and humbled by what I completed. To be clear about what kind of person I am, I am very average. Average height, average weight, average looks, average genetic intelligence. I grew up in a middle class family. No special talents, no special anything.

I wouldn't have even believed someone would even have enough time to do this in a decade. Not only did I have time to do all of this, but I also actually completed much more than listed. Notice that writing a book was not on the list. I'm not a writer. I never liked writing. I never wanted to write. I have never written anything over 55 pages. So much for the nevers! I ended up writing two books. Also, I learned more than two instruments. I learned how to play four different instruments to comfortable levels (playing with my eyes closed for an extended period of time).

I don't believe in lying, it makes our species weak. So, prior to the beginning of nine years ago, I did have some prior knowledge and experience with some on the list. If I had prior knowledge and experience with any on the list, my goal was to learn it on a deeper level than where I already was with it. I had some prior experience and or knowledge of the following; 7, 9, 10, 18.

I did have some prior knowledge of managing wildlife and the places they lived. However, like most things I learned, I learned just enough to get by, never challenging myself to learn the deeper complexities. I stuck to the same methods others used, the easiest way. The easiest way for the biggest short-term gain with complete disregard to long-term problems. The way I managed the forests were backed by my own selfish needs. I was managing the woods for the animals I could benefit from, not managing the woods to benefit as many different animals as I could.

Back then I did not understand or believe in diversity. I wanted to change that way of thinking. I was starting to feel immense guilt for taking and not giving back to those areas that I spent so much time in. I also wanted to learn how many different species of plants and animals would benefit from me *not* focusing my efforts on just one or two species. If I would manage for the benefit of many opposed to the few, what would happen? If I would work with Mother Nature and not against her, what would happen? I was curious, I had to find out.

I figured since planet Earth has been around managing herself for billions of years, it would probably be a good idea to work with her, not against her. My management strategies completely changed. I started using fewer man-made products and fewer modern techniques. I used what was already available in the woods as substitutes to the products I used to have to buy. I enhanced instead of inhibited.

I drastically reduced the amount of man-made products that man has used to manage our forests over the last 100-200 years. I wanted to see the difference. Since the forests, along with their relationships with the soil, insects, plant life, and animal life have been around for billions of years while the products of modern man used for forest and soil management, have only been around for less than 200 years, it may prove to show that the forests and their soils are better off without us interfering.

My new objective for enhancing the biodiversity of a forest while helping the soil get back to its natural state became much clearer. I would spend less time using what man has made in a lab somewhere and spend more time letting Mother Nature do her thing. I was there to help her, not inhibit her. I would slowly change the chemical composition of the soil, gradually returning it to its natural state. Just like building my confidence would benefit many areas of my life, building a healthy, balanced, adaptable soil would benefit many plants and animals since the soil is the foundation of any forest ecosystem.

{4.9} I had next to zero experience or knowledge of all the other goals listed. I did not have many skills, abilities, or deep knowledge of much of anything nine years ago. I may not be at an expert level with some of these, but I have a solid understanding of the core basic fundamental principles of all of them. For example, I have spent the least amount of time learning the complexities of electricity. However, I do have a solid fundamental understanding of how it works. I don't have the fear working with it like I used to either. Am I good enough to be a professional electrician? No. But I am good enough to fix many basic electrical problems in my house. I save several thousand dollars a year by being able to build, fix, and restore.

When I was at my lowest—jobless and on the edge of financial ruin—I had to take any job I could get. Most were well below my previous level of success, as well as the pay. I was feeling the dark pull of life. That pull that can take you down to the darkest, loneliest, and the most dangerous lows of life. I was not going to let myself fall too deep. I had to look at things another way. I may be down for a little while, but over the course of my life, I should be able to minimize those downs if I don't waste any more time feeling sorry for myself and stop making excuses.

I knew this blow to my life was going to hit hard and take me years to recover, but I also knew this: If I continually and consistently worked on being more diversified and more adaptable to changes, then I had a good chance of avoiding those life-altering lows later in life.

{**4.10**} Before we go into the daily nooks and crannies of our life looking for precious minutes here and there, I want to go back to music and my up and down relationship with it. As they say, your most challenging journey will be your most rewarding. This was very true with music. From that list of goals that I was going to embark on nine years ago, I was terrified of learning music. It was so overwhelming, so vast, so many unknowns. My family was not a family who played or listened to music very much at all. Anything to do with music was deeply intimidating. But I had to see. I had to see if I had something musically in me.

I started nine years ago with my first lessons. I needed a lot of help for the first four years. It was painful, yet highly entertaining, despite all of my many failures. My first teacher quit on me after two lessons. Told me, "Some people aren't meant to play music." "Screw That!" I said to myself in my head. Terrible advice. I already knew that was wrong as I wondered how many inadequate teachers said the same things to their students, regardless of what they were teaching them.

Because if you look at it realistically, like everything else, there are only a very few genetic or physical reasons that would prevent some-body from being able to play music.

*To develop a high functioning brain, it's essential to develop both sides of the brain. If you are a left-brained science, math, and analytical person, like me, then working the right brain's creative and expressive side is essential to building a more complex brain. Of course, the opposite is true as well. Working only one side doesn't make you smarter than someone who works both sides of their brain. I'm a natural left-brain. I developed my right brain with music first, then I added the arts (painting, drawing) later. I was shocked to see how many previously closed areas of my brain started to open. The world around me became more understandable and more purposeful. It was intoxicating! Every year, since I started learning the music and the arts, new and incredible skills, ideas, and memories started popping up out of nowhere. Our Human brains have so many hidden treasures waiting for us to discover.*

My second music teacher was thankfully a little more patient than the first one. That second teacher pointed out some interesting flaws I had. She didn't think someone could have a music ear that was this bad. I had no timing and no rhythm. I could not hear if I was on beat or off beat. I could not follow what I was doing, much less play along with someone else. I know I said I had no experience prior to starting nine years ago, but to me, I had less than zero. This is why. I did try to play one instrument for several years before taking lessons. But I only played every few months while never taking the time to learn the basics. I wasn't any good. In fact, my second teacher said that not only did I have a terrible music ear along with a nonexistent understanding of music, I had developed nearly a decade of bad habits. That would set me back years.

That second teacher also said this, "Your determination is extremely high. My other students may be better than you now, but they lack the determination to continually get better." I then asked, "Could you help me learn the basic fundamentals of music and correct my bad habits?" "Yes, I can," my teacher said back. That's all I needed to know.

{4.11} It was painful to learn music from the beginning. Small gains came slowly. Lots of failures, lots of mistakes, lots of cursing. Everything was hard. Nothing came easily or made sense. I might as well have started to explore the unexplored depths of an ocean. That's what it felt like. Everything in learning how to play music felt extremely uncomfortable. But...but, every now and then I would play something the right way at the right time. It sounded great and it felt so damn good! And, I played it. I told myself, "If I can do it once, I can do it twice. If I could do it twice, I could do it ten times, then eventually I could do it 100s of times."

Slowly but surely, each level was reached. My goals were very modest at the beginning. I would have been really happy with just learning 4-5 melodies that I could play by myself, for myself. That was it. Of course, when I felt some of the incredible highs you get when you play music, I wanted more.

After several years of struggling and playing just "okay," but not that good, I hit a crossroads. I was 4-5 years into "playing" two instruments. I was very inconsistent and struggled constantly. I did, however, have several highs throughout the struggles to help keep me going. I plateaued though. I stopped improving. I wanted to get to higher, more complex levels of music, but I was bogged down. Maybe I reached my max, I thought. I felt like I could do more but wasn't sure.

So, I thought about the areas of music that I intentionally or unintentionally avoided. Maybe the answers were where I didn't want to go. As usual, they were. As with most things I learned, I was satisfied taking the easy road. I would choose to work on the areas that were easy to work on and the ones that made me feel good about myself. I would choose to avoid the areas that were harder to work on and made me feel bad about myself. My goals from the beginning were superficially based. I cared far more about how I looked at playing music instead of how I sounded. I cared more about how much admiration I would get rather than challenging myself. I initially wanted the quickest, easiest way to get good at something.So of course I hit a wall. The second I stopped challenging myself and pushing to continually work on the things I struggled with rather than work on the things I was already good at, was the second I became much closer to that wall.

I remember my teacher telling me that my timing was especially bad, and in music, without timing, you don't have much to build on. No matter where I looked in life, a poorly built foundation always resulted in many problems later. I was instructed several times to work on a metronome (a basic device that emits a pattern of beeps in a certain tempo that you play your instrument along with). It's one of the most basic, fundamental tools and drills you can use to build a good musical ear foundation. I thought I was above that kind of practice. And I hated it. I hated it more than anything in music. I also thought that I was too cool to use something so basic. I just knew I could get to higher, more complex levels of playing music without working on basic, fundamental skills.

It turned out I was really wrong on that one. I was okay with being just an average musician since my history with music was so terrible. Music is the most challenging and humbling thing I have ever tried to learn. I hate quitting, and rarely do it, but this wall was frustrating me to new levels. There were only two times throughout that list of goals that I thought about quitting. Both were because of music.

And both times, after going back to that basic, fundamental shit that I hated so much, it would work. It would get me out of my quitting attitude. And it would also get me through nearly every wall or obstacle I reached in music. I remember telling myself, "Just try and play along to the metronome for five minutes, that's it."

Within 3-4 weeks of doing this, something so damn cool started happening. My ears started correcting my sloppiness on their own. My notes and changes tightened up. I was playing more controlled. I was playing new melodies. Melodies that I couldn't even play a few weeks earlier. I couldn't believe it. I was hooked!

{4.12} After getting a little better at the fundamentals of music, I started adding instruments to the list. If I could learn two, why not more? Unfortunately, as life goes, time that I used to have more of was in decline. I did not want to lose what I worked so hard to get to but I still wanted to learn more instruments, even if I had less time...

*Time for a new plan...*

What would I do if I couldn't physically get better at something? How could I get better at a musical instrument if I physically wouldn't be able to hold it and use it as much as I needed to? This would get frustrating many times over until I figured out the answer was already in my head. In fact, it was my head, or at least, what's in it. I could keep up with my skills, even if only in my head. Then when I had time, I would catch the physical part up. Years prior I was mainly working only on the physical aspects of the skills I was trying to gain.

*Incorporating the mind and the brain with the physical skills will get our brain to higher levels of understanding and control.*

I had to continually talk to my mind and get it out of the way so the brain could do its work. If I combined thousands of hours of physical repetitions combined with mental repetitions, what would happen to my skills?

Since I was losing the time I had available to work on the physical aspects of music, I had to put more emphasis on the mental aspect. It took me doing something I rarely did and something that I wasn't comfortable with; thinking about something I just finished doing and kept thinking about it until it clicked on a comfortable level of understanding. It's similar to walking out of class and you keep thinking about what the teacher was saying. You keep thinking about it for a few minutes while you try to figure out the meaning. Or the opposite, when you walk out of class and never give a second thought to what the teacher was saying. It's pretty easy to figure out which brain would develop more than the other.

So instead of just listening to a song, I began to actively participate in the song, in my head anyway. I was able to keep my skills sharp under the radar even in a room full of people. As long as there was music in the background, I could make use of that time. While others around me would be knee-deep in life-wasting gossip and dramas, I was pretending I was the one playing the individual instruments in the background, in my head, where no one knew anything.

As challenging as music was, I kept doing it. Slowly but surely, things would change. It was weird and inspiring all at the same time. For months nothing changed, nothing new was played. Then one day out of nowhere...it happened. The seemingly impossible...happened. I could, all of a sudden, do what I never thought I could do. I could play free and on time. The feelings I would get those days were some of the best feelings I have ever felt, even as a kid. Actually, those incredible feelings I would get from music were in many ways exceeding the incredible feelings I had as a kid. **Those days of huge musical breakthroughs will go down as some of the very best days of my life!**

*I was once told that I should never play music.*

Our brains are sneaky. They will be working on advancing our skills "behind the scenes" for quite a while until one day, it all comes together. Those were some of my happiest and proudest days of my life. And I was an adult. I remember several times looking down at my body shocked that I was playing that sound coming out of those instruments. I now believed how powerful it was to imagine myself playing those instruments in my head to the music around me.

For me, there was no denying it anymore. The highest and deepest levels of our gifts and abilities are hidden, yet waiting to be found and released. The combination of consistently working on both the physical and mental skills in different and creative ways can unleash something spectacular inside each of us.

{4.13} Another helpful mental change I made was removing unnecessary, life-inhibiting man-made rules in just about everything I tried to learn. Especially when it came to Music and the Arts. There really are no rules in Music and Art. If you like it, then do it like that. And keep it for your personal collection. Who cares what other people think about what you do or what you create? What you create is for you.

*If a bird with a very small brain can sing perfect and beautiful songs without knowing notes, chords, measures, or any other musical rules, why can't most of us do that? A bird's songs are free of self-made restrictions.*

Who cares if you play with the proper form or technique? Just play or create what makes you happy. The form and techniques will work themselves out if you work toward free creativity. If you can tap your finger consistently to a beat, you can play music. Trying to stick to all the rules of music was daunting and frustrating for me. Every musician I talked to had their own set of rules. Rules, rules, more rules! I thought that music and art were wide open freedoms of expression? Nope! As usual, when us Humans are involved, unnecessary, made up laws and rules show up. Even music and art. No matter who I talked to about music, no matter their level of experience, very few of them played or created freely without some kind of personal made-up rule they adhered to.

We Humans love rules. I don't know why. It holds back our entire species. I was learning music the first five or six years, just like I did everything else, with lots of self-imposed rules. I was told you had to hold the instrument this way, hold it that way, you should have this many measures here and this many there, you need minor and major chords for songs, this is that way, that is this way...blah...blah...blah! More exhausting Human behaviors. More life-sucking rules in my life. And now more rules in music. Not for me, not anymore.

Something like plumbing is different. Rules are needed. Because plumbing deals with the laws of nature. Try not following the rules when sealing the joints of two connecting pipes and watch what happens. Water will find and expose any weak spots. Common sense plumbing rules are necessary. Unnecessary life-sucking rules in Music and the Arts are not.

As I discarded more and more self-inhibiting made-up rules, music (and life in general) became much more enjoyable. I felt less pressure...

*I felt more free...*

{4.14} Everything we just learned about music can be applied to virtually everything in our daily lives that we want to improve. Parenting, cooking, shopping, gardening, carpentry, repairing and restoring things, exercising, dieting, our career, our education, athletics, any hobby, etc...

*1. Master the fundamentals over time, bit by bit (mental, emotional, and physical).*

*2. Experiment on doing a wide variety of things.*

*3. Throw out self-inhibiting, self-imposed, man-made rules and beliefs.*
*4. Don't stop, ever...just a little at a time.*
*5. That's pretty much it...*

The writing of this book is a good example of all of this. Several years ago, I had zero intentions of writing any book. But as time went on, my personality changes were starting to make real life-changing changes. I thought it would be really selfish if I didn't at least try to help others. I know I'm like most of everyone else, and I figured if some of this was helping me, why not write it down? Maybe others can find their own personal freedom through some of what I'm going through.

But I was years away from having the time to sit and write. However, during those years I was waiting to write, I spent several thousand hours *thinking* about everything in this book. Slowly but surely, the understanding would come. Then the words for how to explain what I was experiencing would eventually come.

I thought about all of this a lot. I was curious. I was curious about our species. I was curious as to what we may be capable of.

That's the next chapter...

# Chapter 5

# Our Species and the Faults We Possess

{5.1} As hard as it is to sometimes think about, we are a species. We are, all eight billion of us, a single species. Every species that has ever existed on this planet has good qualities as well as not so good. We have never been more of a species as we are now. We are mostly all connected. You can be anywhere on Earth in a relatively short period of time. You can communicate with almost anyone on Earth in a very short period of time.

As with most species, our species has many good qualities. And like most species, we have some qualities that are dangerous and toxic. Most of our toxic and dangerous qualities are eerily similar to other species. Our best and worst qualities and behaviors can be found among a countless number of other species.

_Examples:_ Even something as tangible as STDs (sexually transmitted diseases) are not just found in our species. Many animals can get

STDs, like koalas contracting chlamydia and chimpanzees contracting HIV. But those are just physical.

Behavioral examples are plenty. Behaviors are behaviors, and it doesn't matter what kind of creature does them. Our Human behaviors, most of them anyway, can be found in exhausting repetition throughout the animal kingdom; physical abuse, sexual abuse, dominating and controlling others, inequality, lying, laziness, masturbation, gay, lesbian, stealing, cheating, rape, murder, incest, addictions, molestation of the young, neglecting their babies. All of these behaviors plus more are found throughout the animal kingdom.

*- Male roosters _raping_ female hens.*
*- Gangs of young male roosters _raping_ and _murdering_ a young hen then leaving her body as a piece of trash.*
*- Wallabies letting their babies go hungry (_neglect_) until they get their "fix" (_addiction_) on poppy seeds in the poppy seed fields.*
*- Fish within coral reefs _stealing_ rocks from their neighbor to build their house without doing the hard work (_lazy_).*
*- Just about every animal species has _gay_ and _lesbian_ behaviors within them. Two male dogs licking each other between the legs.*
*- A lion killing and crushing the head of a cheetah that it never intended to eat or use for anything. That's _murder_.*
*- Etc...etc...etc...etc...etc...etc...*

So, what then really separates us from the other animals that live around us? Very little in my opinion.

Except for one aspect. We are the first species ever to develop the ability and foresight to rise above the genetically and environmentally embedded behaviors that virtually every other species are driven by. Or at least we should be able to. We should be the one species who is capable of avoiding these toxic animal behaviors that continually hold our species back. Unfortunately however, throughout the history of our species, we continue to behave in highly destructive patterns that so many lower animals do all the time. As we know by now there are countless stories of deplorable human behaviors since the beginning of our time on this planet. Those deeply deplorable human behaviors are still being passed down to every generation of our kids.

But shouldn't we be behaving differently than lower animals? Yes, we should and many of us do but many more of us do not. Too many of us do whatever we want whenever we want without any regard to long-term outcome. Way too many of us Humans make life more and more challenging for ourselves, our families, and our communities. Way too many of us fall into familiar patterns of behaviors seen over and over again in lower animals.

For example, why is it so common for our species to try and control and dominate others around us?

Because that's what most other living things are built to do, whether a plant, an insect, a fungus, a bacterium, or us; dominate and control your environment, which includes others living around you.

It may work with other species, but it definitely does not work for ours. If any of us Humans try to control and dominate others around us, problems are guaranteed to arise. We are supposed to be the species to overcome the debilitating behaviors that other species may not be able to overcome.

Why then? Why does our species continually fall into the same behavioral patterns that lower species fall into?

If we do not or cannot out-think destructive natural animal behaviors then we become them and they will eventually take us down.

It also does not matter how we got on this planet, it matters only how we adapt to and take care of our home. If there is a Creator, it still does not matter. We still have to take care of the home He, She, or It has given us. Could you imagine the conversation we would have to have with our Creator after they saw what we have become, how we treat each other and what we did and are doing to an entire planet? I'm pretty sure the Creator would even be surprised by how only one species can destroy an entire planet and then blame everyone and everything else for the damage.

Or what about our species finally meeting aliens from another galaxy? What would they think of us once they met us and got to know us and our habits?

{5.2} Locked into a single way of living or believing defines most of our species. As with virtually all living systems, diversity is one of the Laws of Nature that drives thriving ecosystems. It is one of the most absolute ways to increase productivity, strength, and resilience within any ecosystem, being adaptable with a high amount of diversity. The more diverse something is, the more successful they are over long-periods of time. The same goes for how we respond to life's challenges. Should we respond to what happens to us the same way every time? Or should we adapt our responses to each unique situation?

Even most lower animals have a diversity of responses. What happens when two male dogs see each other for the first time? They size each other up and make a calculated decision whether to engage in an energy-expensive physical fight. Some will show their teeth and raise their body hair in an attempt to back-down the other dog in hopes of not physically engaging. They are *choosing* which option is beneficial or not-so beneficial. They are choosing to vary their responses depending on their situation.

Countless times I've heard people say, "Nobody will ever cross me!" "Nobody" crosses you? Nobody is a definitive word. If used, it automatically puts you into a very tight, restricted, stressful corner. We have given ourselves one option for how to respond to someone who "crosses" us. And this one option can lead to an exhaustive, wasteful lifestyle. Many people and many situations we encounter throughout life are not worth the time and energy we will lose. Giving ourselves multiple types of responses gives us more flexibility and adaptability in our responses, which will eventually lead to a more dynamic, complex, problem-solving brain.

It's almost always in the subtleties of daily life where we build either a complex problem-solving brain or a simple problem-creating brain. Of course, there will be a few major events in our lives that help shape our brain and minds, but for the most part, it's the accumulation of many, many, many repeated daily activities that drive the construction of our Human brains and minds.

And you and I have tremendous control over the direction in which we build our brain and our minds. There are really only three ways in which to build the brain, any brain, any animal brain.

*1. We can build our brain into a powerful, problem-solving, highly creative brain that makes our lives easier. (positive energy)*
*2. We can build our brain onto a weak, uncreative, problem-creating brain that makes our lives more challenging. (negative energy)*
*3. We can do nothing and succumb to whatever the brain becomes depending highly on the environment the brain developed in. (neutral energy)*

When we build up our brains on our own, the benefits are too many to count. We become less dependent on others, which gives us more freedom. When we give our minds and brains unrestricted freedom of thought, that is the exact time they start to become a highly creative, undeniable problem-solver.

If we all have the same chance to develop a powerful, problem-solving brain, why do so many of us continually fall into the two less-desirable ways to build our brain (numbers 2 and 3)? Before we get into how we create problem-creating brains, let's figure out how we can build or not build those three types of brains.

### *Brain #1: The Creative and Problem-Solving Brain:*

*- Has been exposed to real-life challenges.*

*- Is surrounded by an unbiased open mind.*

*- Is a continuous learner of diverse information, new and old.*

*- Does not take the easy way out.*

*- Possesses full accountability for its mistakes.*

*- Devises plans to deal with life's problems in life-enhancing ways.*

*- Continually questions the reactions and the decisions the mind surrounding it makes.*

### *Brain #2: The Uncreative and Problem-Creating Brain:*

*- Continually takes the easy way out.*

*- Has not been exposed to real-life challenges.*

*- Continually blames others for everything.*

*- Has no plans to deal with problems and therefore depends heavily on others to fix them.*

*- Surrounded by a closed mind that causes more problems than it solves.*

*- Devises plans that may spark short-term success along with more long-term problems to later follow.*

### *Brain #3: The Do-Nothing Brain:*

*- Has been protected and hid from real-life challenges.*

*- Tends to follow whatever other people do so as to be accepted.*

*- Learns just enough to get a degree or a job, then pretty much stops learning.*

*- Is content with the limited knowledge it contains.*

*- Is surrounded by a biased, weak mind that filters out most useful information.*

*- Rarely questions the reactions and decisions the mind surrounding it makes.*

{5.3} Consider this analogy. Animal behavior changes dramatically when their lives become threatened or challenged. If you ever get the chance, closely observe the behavioral differences within the same species when their lives are threatened versus when they are not. The unthreatened animals become completely different animals when their lives are threatened.

Take, for example, an un-hunted population of wild hogs that becomes a hunted population. If I'm a hog, or any living thing for that matter, that is born into an environment with an abundance of food, secure cover, along with no predators after me, I may feel safer and more relaxed than a hog that's born into the opposite. Even if there was an abundance of food, if something was trying to kill us while we ate, I'm pretty sure our behavioral approach to getting the food would change.

I've seen these scenarios play out many times. I can almost walk right up to wild animals that are not hunted by us or other animals (like a park effect). They almost become dumb. Their ability to solve problems is nearly lost. They become routine. Same travel routes every day. If a predator would happen to show up, it would be easy pickings for them. Dumb animals who can't adapt fast enough don't survive long.

Something quite interesting happens when their lives become threatened, however. Their behavior changes. They become more observant, they become more methodical in their approach to going anywhere. They become exceptionally more intelligent in their decision-making. They become a different animal. They completely stop their lazy, haphazard walks through the forests. They try to learn the habits of those who try to eat it. They adapt their lifestyle in a highly intelligent way. They begin to max out their intelligence to the highest order. To me, it became rather simple and clear, the unchallenged brain was and is simple to overcome and manipulate. The challenged, intelligent brain is not.

We see this play out over and over and again and again in our very own species. Unbiasedly observe the behavioral patterns of our species and you will begin to see similar patterns. Don't take my word for it. Observe, learn, and decide on your own.

Any of us who are unprepared to handle life's challenges continually fall victim to others around us. Adults or kids who are sheltered from real-life challenges simply do not have the chance to develop the skills needed to handle our everyday challenges.

It's not like us Humans will be hunted any time soon, so how does this apply to us? There are many examples of this throughout our species. I'll use a simple analogy that unfolds every day in classrooms across our planet.

### <u>Classroom A</u>

1. Encourages students to stick to book material.
2. Does not promote creativity.
3. Tells students this is the way it's always been so don't question it, just learn it.
4. Administers tests that can be passed with simple memorization.

5. Challenges students with many standardized tests cluttered with superficial knowledge.

6. Allows failing students to pass with minimal resistance.

7. Puts more emphasis on grades than deep, connective knowledge.

8. High emphasis on following a schedule.

OR...


**Classroom B**

1. Encourages students to explore thoughts and ideas outside of the book.

2. Promotes creative thinking.

3. Tells students its ok to question.

4. Administers tests that will be failed if one memorizes.

5. Challenges students to understand and build deep, connective knowledge.

6. Fails students who fail to learn the material properly.

7. Puts more emphasis on deep knowledge gained over grades.

8. Low emphasis on following a schedule.


Again, conduct your own research and observations, don't take just mine. Your best brain is built by learning things with your own eyes, nose, ears, hands, mind, and brain. Just because we watch somebody else doing something, it doesn't mean our own brain fully programs it into us. We must *do* as well.

What would become of these kids (in those two classrooms) who would eventually turn into adults?


{5.4} Are we that different from other species? Why do we think we are so "special"? Why do we continuously think we are so much greater than all the other species of Earth?

How long have we been here compared to other species? In that sense, we are a juvenile species. We are one of the youngest species on Earth right now. On top of that, we are the first species to accomplish complex communications and dynamic endeavors that no other species has even come close to. Our species has accomplished incredible feats that no other species has even come close to. So, does that make us more "special" than all the other species?

As one of the youngest species, we are making catastrophic mistakes. As we are the most inventive and entrepreneurial species to ever exist, we are also the most damaging and dangerous species to ever exist. We continue to exploit, alter, and damage the very surroundings that we depend on to exist.

Every species ever, before us and during our time here, depends on reading and responding to their surroundings, without words. They (plants, insects, animals) must adapt and figure out their surroundings without words. How? They feel. They feel, learn, adapt, and begin to understand their surroundings without words. How? How can all other species do this and then all of a sudden, *our* species cannot? Well, not all of our species fails at recognizing, dealing with, and using "feel" to navigate through life. The young of our species use it extensively. The young of our species don't completely understand language, so they use their ability to "feel" their environment to navigate through their first part of life.

**The only group of living things that have abandoned their ability to "feel" their environment are Human adults.**

How? How can all other species, including the young of our species, do this and then suddenly, as we become adults, it's no longer important? That's nonsense, of course we can. We are not that different all of sudden. It may be easy to talk or manipulate our way out of life's challenging situations without really dealing with them in the short term, but it is destroying us in the long-term.

If every other species that has ever existed on this planet has had to adapt and modify its behavior to its ever-changing environment, why do we think all of a sudden our species is so special that we can continually modify our environment without adapting our behavior? We are doing the exact opposite of every other species, ever. Our species is the perfect analogy for the "Forcing a Square Peg in a Round Hole." We continually modify our man-made laws with disregard to the Natural Laws of Nature.

Of all the successful Humans I have observed, one thing was very clear, they continuously and consistently worked *with* the Natural Laws of our planet, not *against* them. Less emphasis was put on adhering to man-made, made up laws and rules. A few man-made examples of rules that frustrate our lives that have zero meaning:

**1. _Fashion rules_** - Who really cares what you wear or when you wear it? Our species has actually killed each other because of the pointless "rules" of fashion.

**2. _Relationship rules_** - Not everyone is built for dating and marriage. Some of our species thrives on being single. Pretty much any rule that our partners in any relationship give us are wasteful and pointless. Successful Humans live by very few self-imposed, man-made rules and they sure don't waste time in relationships that have rules built into them by the other person.

Quick examples of how modern Humans ignore the Natural Laws of Nature in expense for what we think it should be:
- *Our Diet. Refer back to Chapter 3 for great detail of how we have destroyed our millions-year-old species' diet.*

*- Our species is so arrogant that we think we can modify food into something that our species, and our millions-year-old digestive system, have never seen before and then claim that it is good for us over time.*
*- Ask yourself: What has our species been eating for the last few million years we've been here?*
*- Modern man-made food has only been around for less than 150 years.*
*- What was the food like for our ancestors before modern food came around?*

What if our species *is* 4.5 million years old? For all but 150 years or so our species has been eating food that is different from what we eat now. Before grocery stores, our species' diet was dominated by whatever was available on the planet at that time. This is where we can see the separation between man-made laws and the Laws of Nature. Laws of Nature have never and may never change and have been here for billions of years. Man-made rules and laws change continually and have been here for a few hundred years.

Going back to the food example, we see that our species has been eating foods following the Laws of Nature 99.999% of our existence and we have only been consuming modern foods for 0.0001% of our existence. Creating easy-to-make, highly automated modern foods during the last 0.0001% of our species existence is one more example of a "Forcing a Square Peg into a Round Hole" type species.

We can tell ourselves whatever we want about the foods we put into our mouths (or anything else in our life), but the reality of the Natural Laws will eventually express themselves. If our organ systems (like our digestive system), as a single species, have been adapting to and performing at certain levels when exposed to a "millions of years old" diet, what do we think will happen to our overall health when we dramatically alter the human diet in less than 150 years?

*We are a young, naive species with much to learn. We continuously think that we can bypass the Laws of Nature and make up our own. We dangerously think that new ideas are better than the old ideas. One of our species' most incredible characteristics, inventing new things, is also one of our most destructive.*

{5.5} But our greatest traits are also some of our worst. Sometimes our greatest traits can become our most destructive, it just depends how we choose to use them. So many of us throughout the history of our existence continue to rely on new ideas to solve old problems. Of course, new ideas should be welcomed and considered as problem solvers, but we should not dismiss old ideas and methods. New inventions and ideas are exciting and sometimes more efficient than old ideas and inventions. However, we should take reality for what it is instead of making it fit to whatever we want it to. New gadgets, new ideas, new inventions may improve our lives but it's never a good idea to completely abandon all other ideas. Variety right here again reigns King.

I'm a victim of this as well. New technology is always better than old, right? Anything that we invented now is better than anything that was invented in the 1980s, right? This was a restrictive way of thinking for me and can be for anybody who wants to develop a highly intelligent brain. This way of thinking always led me to looking for something new instead of just going with what works.

Some of our species' inventions have been very helpful to our existence, while some of our inventions have just set us back.

**Some basic Human skills that allow us personal freedom:**
*1. Selecting, preparing, and cooking our own food.*

2. *Fixing/Building/Repairing/Restoring.*

3. *Wide-Open Mind.*

4. *Lots of variety in virtually everything.*

5. *Able to treat many common ailments ourselves.*

6. *Able to travel and navigate directions on our own.*

7. *Being able to let go and move on when appropriate.*

8. *Self-built inner confidence...*

9. *Long-term vision.*

10. *Being able to accept and understand those who are different from us.*

We live in a time that is striving to make our lives easier, but are we? If I use a new modern invention that saves me a little time in the short-term but diminishes my overall skills over time in the long-term, is it worth it?

Washing Machine? Dishwasher? Those are perfect examples of inventions that save us time but do *not* diminish our skills. But what about our food? There is a big difference between families who can cook but don't have the time to cook versus families that do not know how to cook.

Just in the last few years there has been a shift toward more prepared meals delivered right to our door. On the surface, it sounds incredible, one less thing I have to do. I can press a few buttons and have a full-course meal delivered to my family. Who doesn't want that? But again, follow and observe the families who rely *heavily* on these types of services. Short-term help for long-term...what? Every skill we fail to maintain over the course of our lives brings us closer and closer to being controlled by others.

By giving into the new, easy way to feed me and my family, I have diminished my own skills. And I have also become very dependent on others for me and my family's food.

{5.6} Do you ever wonder what's wrong with our species? Why does this generation of our species keep falling into the same cracks that every other generation of Humans have also fallen into? Every generation since the beginning of our species seems to have the same problems; poverty, inequality, hate, greed, pollution, violence, etc…

Every generation seems to think that their answers to our problems are almost universally better than their ancestors. New answers to the same old problems. New and novel ideas in the present seem to hold such a high value over older ideas.

What is our obsession with always having to one-up the previous? It's one of our major downfalls as a species. Of course, some new and novel ideas are better than the old, but it's the theory behind our overall thought process that will hinder our development as an individual or as a species.

If I rely heavily on new ideas or inventions and continue to cast aside anything old, I'm turning portions of my brain off and closed to using any past information. I am restricting and suffocating my own brain from a large amount of information. I am making myself dumber and more dependent on others when I restrict myself from thinking "outside the box."

The other way of thinking is not good either. If we heavily rely on using old, seemingly outdated ideas and inventions without giving any thoughts to new ideas and inventions; then we will still make our brains dumber and more dependent on others.

*It really does not matter which side we are on; we are causing damage to ourselves as we are making our lives so much more difficult when we rely too much on one way of thinking. Individuals, families, communities, cultures, and countries that live with a consistently closed mind will always struggle throughout their existence. It's our own fault, we have blocked our own brain from developing into a powerful problem-solving brain.*

Developing a close-minded lifestyle puts you into a figurative corner of the room. I imagine myself stuck in an inside corner of a room. I cannot move behind me. I cannot move to the left or to the right. I can only move forward. I have left myself with one move, one option. I gave myself one option out of the possible four options. Out of 100% of options, I gave myself only 25% of that by restricting my options because of my own narrow-minded beliefs.

In this simple analogy, we can only control 25% of our movement. That is what my one-way, restrictive thinking was constantly doing to me. Getting myself stuck in a corner where I only gave myself one way out. In reality, if we closely observe our species, those that continually restrict their ability to make a wide variety of choices, most likely have much less than 25% control over their life.

How could we? If I try to solve all of my problems the same way and never try any other way, then I have given up most of my decision-making to others. We have given up one of the most prized Human characteristics; our freedom of having an extensive library of ideas, reactions, solutions, and emotions that are highly diverse and adaptive.

*For myself, this concept change I allowed in my mind and my brain was one of the more crucial decisions I ever made in my head. It finally made sense, "Variety is the Spice of Life." Variety, however, is so much more than just a "spice" of life. It is the absolute backbone of virtually all living systems.*

Back to variety in my own head and how it became life changing. I found when I was inflexible with my ideas and beliefs, my life would automatically become more stressful, more difficult, and less fun. I was trying to force a "square peg into a round hole" if you will. My health also took a dive. Higher blood pressure, increased anxiety, unbalanced erratic thoughts, etc. Then my mental behavior would change as well. If I could not get others to see my way, then I would go to other, not so endearing, tactics like lying, cheating, manipulation, hurtful words and actions, etc...

I used to never have a variety of thoughts and ideas. I always put myself into a theoretical corner. One idea, one thought, one direction to go. It was all my fault. I have blamed everyone and everything for my problems while giving myself only one way to go. I gave myself no other options because I continually chose to solve my problems the same way.

### {5.7} *Another Human Species Fault:*
*Lack of Diversity and Adaptability*

Before I decided to fully invest my time into adding more variety in my life, I first decided to do lots of observation of non-human living systems. "Variety is the spice of life" doesn't just say that it applies to human life. If this potential Law of Nature were to hold up, variety should be found in other life-systems, right?

Well, it didn't take very long, variety was found everywhere I looked. Well at least I found a high degree of variety in the healthy systems. The unhealthy systems had very little variety of anything. It became clear to me how important variety and diversity was. It's one of the essential components for all successful life forms. Too many of our species fail to realize this critically important component of our existence. This one characteristic, if used properly, could exponentially increase one's individual intelligence.

For more than a decade, I've been observing the value of diversity and variety throughout as many different living systems as I could. I highly encourage you to allow your brain and mind to take it all in as well.

For my personal observations, this is what I saw unfold. I unbiasedly observed as many different living systems as I could to see if I could pick up any patterns. I'll just talk about a few to keep it short.

From fields to forests, oceans to lakes, to families, to cities, to cultures, to gut bacteria. To me, it all came down to a very simple concept. Variety and diversity are the absolute pillars and the "middle links" in the chain. ***Middle links are the most important links within a chain, if they break, the entire chain may fall apart. If an end link breaks, the rest of the chain may not be affected.*** Same with virtually all living systems. The vast majority of living systems that have low diversity and low variety are very unsuccessful and would eventually crash because of their limited options.

A diverse field or forest has lots of different types of insects, birds, reptiles, and mammals. A field or forest lacking variety may hold only a few different plant species with very few insects and most likely no reptiles or mammals.

A few plant species attract much fewer varieties of insects, and birds. These ecosystems perform at low levels and are in constant struggle. They become dangerously dependent on only a few resources. Same goes for bodies of water, no matter the size. Living systems are much stronger when they have a diversity of options. The constant life struggle was not found like it was in the low diverse systems.

What about our gut bacteria and its ecosystem? I read as much as I could on this subject from as many different perspectives and fields of study that I could, but it wasn't satisfying enough. This type of observation needed to be done internally. I had to see it for myself using my own gut bacteria.

First though, bacteria, who are unseen by the naked eye, seem to be quite important to us and how our bodies work. Bacterial cells in us and on us outnumber our own body cells 10 to 1. They perform countless beneficial jobs in us and on us all the time. Five pounds of an average human body is made up of microscopic bacteria. Most of the internal ones are found in the lower parts of the large intestine (colon). Also, and quite importantly, these bacteria living in our lower abdominal region are in constant communication with our brain. These bacteria that help run us are incredibly smart and adaptable. It's safe to say, without them, we do not exist.

But are they strong in just sheer numbers, or does the variety of bacteria matter? If we had 10 billion bacteria made up of only two types versus 10 billion bacteria made up of 100 different types—with each type having the ability to perform its own unique job—the answer seemed pretty clear after I thought that through. But I still wanted to see it and feel it myself.

I was going to have to try several different diets over an extended period of time. It takes approximately 8-12 months to change and adapt our Gut Bacteria to most new diets.

So to me, trying a new diet for a few weeks or a few months was not going to cut it. I kept my diet self-testing concept pretty simple. I based my diets on the percentage of natural foods (little to no altering from its natural state) versus unnatural foods (processed foods far away from its natural state).

*Chapter 3* covers all of this in much more detail. I'll keep it short here. My dominant adult diet was 75% unnatural foods and 25% natural foods. I took a personal unbiased assessment of my short and long-term ailments, from minor to major and any aches and pains.

*I also tried the ...*
- *75% natural and 25% unnatural diet.*
- *90% natural and 10% unnatural diet.*
- *100% natural and 0% unnatural diet.*

The only one I did not try for several years was the 100% natural and 0% unnatural diet. Maybe if I would have the 100% diet in a different order and have been more prepared it may have been different. But I felt, for my life, the 100% diet was a little unnecessary and way too restrictive. There was no wiggle room and not enough freedom. I was, however, feeling really good on that diet. That diet will maximize and enhance everything good in you.

But I wanted my gut bacteria to be more adaptable and diversified so they would be able to handle it when I could not eat an all-natural (100%) diet. For me and my lifestyle, the sweet spot diet was the 90% natural and 10% unnatural. I never gave up sweets, I actually increased the diversity of sweets I ate, just kept them at a very low percentage of my overall diet.

As with most living systems, diversity was the key. The diverse diet that our species has been evolving with the last few million years was slowly but surely correcting my physical ailments that were continually building up over the previous years. The diversity of my gut bacteria now developing in my gut were able to handle a wider diversity of foods and my body was starting to show incredible results.

*Chapter 3* has more than what we discuss here but I'll quickly break down a few of the health benefits I was seeing and feeling as my gut bacteria started to change.

## 10-12 months into the 90% natural and 10% unnatural Diet:
- *My chronically inflamed shoulder and knee joints became almost completely free of burning pain. - (Inflamed, painful joints have not returned in nine years)*

## 2-3 years into Diet:
- *Brain functions increased as I aged.*
- *More clarity in my thoughts.*
- *Digestive problems were infrequent and minimal.*

## 4-5 years into Diet:
- *The return of my immune system.*
- *Was beginning to go 2-3 full calendar years without a day of sickness. When sick, it was rarely more than 48 hours.*

{5.8} Even in the microscopic world, diversity and variety reigned king. Diversity led to living things having adaptability to the changes around them. Variety and adaptability kept ecosystems out of trouble, at least for long periods of time. Most ecosystems would behave this way.

*Within us, a high degree of diversity and adaptability in our minds and brains gives us the power to not be controlled and held back by others.*

It didn't matter where I looked, diversity and adaptability gave more options. No matter where I looked, more options continually kept species out of that tight, close-quartered, limited-options corner. Balanced, highly diverse ecosystems have plenty of options to go to during times of stress. They collapse at a much lower rate than the unbalanced, less diverse ones.

After studying and observing the same pattern in virtually all species, I wondered, "Do we perform better as a species with high diversity and high adaptability as well?" Would we have less problems as a species if we finally embraced diversity and adaptability?

*We may be the only species in the history of Earth that struggles to adapt to its environment. We modify our surroundings way more than we adapt to them.*

As I quietly and unbiasedly observed families, neighborhoods, cities, states, and countries with this diversity and adaptability in mind, I asked myself, "Would we lean toward the immensely beneficial qualities that they give us, or would we ignore them as being unnecessary for an advanced species?"

As with most, I found both within our species. After years and years of observing myself and my actions along with others around me, I started feeling really stupid. I was definitely low in both adaptability and diversity. I was way too simple and single minded, and I rarely changed or challenged my initial thoughts and beliefs. I possessed a strict, restrictive mind who was continually putting myself into a tight inner corner with limited options. No wonder I was so fearful; I gave myself so few options to be able to handle much of anything in life.

{5.9} Back to families and cities. Does diversity and adaptability have much to do with the successes and failures of these as well? First off, unbiased, non-judgmental observing was quite challenging for me. This is no doubt an epigenetically induced type of judgment. *(Epigenetics- environmental control of our genes in our DNA that can be changed throughout our life by our decisions, our actions and our environments. Think of our diet that we chose changing our genes over time)*. Thousands and thousands of generations of overly and unnecessarily judgmental Humans judging the differences between them. Us Humans have been judging each other from the beginning. What did we think was going to happen to us now? Virtually all animals pre-judge another before engaging. We are no different. But again, shouldn't *we* be the species that overcomes this immensely debilitating trait?

I had to continually remind myself against biased pre-judgement. What helped me? If I was critical of someone else, I would immediately turn that critique and criticism back on me. After I did that a few times I quickly realized that I wasn't so perfect after all.

The more critical I was of myself, the more I found it easier to be an unbiased observer of others. As I began to look for patterns of success and failures in our species, I needed to define what a successful Human would be like. I needed to be careful with how I defined successful Human Beings.

*Labeling and defining someone is another type of restrictive, low-level brain behavior.*

I decided on some rather broad classifications. I also based my observations on living factors. For example, money is made-up by our species. No us, no money. Although we have to have it in our modern world, it is not living, and it has not evolved with us for millions of years. Also, Humans can have lots of money and be artificially successful at the same time being not so successful at being a Human. Money does not guarantee us a successful life on Earth. It can no doubt ease some of our modern life's stresses, but it is far from a cure-all. It worked well not factoring in money or prestige or someone's position of power. Any one of us can have a highly successful life without being wealthy, even though most of our species, including me for a very long time, continually put money very high on the priority list of life.

*Of course, money, income, and the economy are important, and we should be successful at those, but they only make up a very small portion of what our species really is and what we have to offer.*

The most successful individuals, families, cities, countries, and cultures within our species have mastered that one idea. Money does not dominate their decision making. It can't dominate our decision making if we are diverse and adaptable. Any *one* thought or idea, good or bad, should never dominate us and control our life or decision-making. Stuck in a corner with only one way out is not intelligent or successful. Successful individuals and families I observed were rarely stuck in a corner. They usually, almost always, gave themselves many options to get out of any challenge they may encounter throughout life.

{5.10} Before I could fully "define" the successful, the ones I observed gave me the direction and answers I needed. Once I took the superficial "success" out of our species, my definition of what a successful Human would be like was becoming clearer and clearer.

Right off the bat I noticed how I felt different when being around the ones that seem to have life figured out; they were happy, balanced, and peaceful. They made me feel good when I was around them. They raised my energy level. They were not rich, powerful, or famous. They were just incredible individuals living among us. I owe this book to people like them. Without these dynamic, incredible Human beings to watch and learn from, there is no book.

I wanted to know how they were doing it. Even if their world seemed to be falling apart around them, they kept their heads up and kept moving forward while still finding the simple joys in life to carry them through. There had to be patterns, similarities between these types of people, right?

Over time, patterns and certain qualities continually showed up, whether in individuals, families, or cultures. For one, the lows of life did not knock these people as far down as the rest of us. No matter how disastrous or challenging life had become, they fell, but didn't fall far nor did they stay down for long periods of time. It was incredible to watch. They were inspiring. I've also witnessed some people and some families fall for much lesser types of challenges in life and sometimes never recover. I witnessed many times how family genetics, a family's power, money, or prestige could not even spare them from the lows of life. The overall outcome was vastly different when it came to comparing families built on superficial success versus families built on real Human successes.

Another factor began to show itself between successful and unsuccessful individuals, families, and cultures. No matter if poor, middle-class, or wealthy; problems, drama, chaos, and high stress were nearly always present when superficial short-term decisions took priority over common sense long-term decisions. Decisions that were mostly based on short-term success with little regard to how those decisions would negatively affect their own future success.

Successful Humans have such an open mind loaded with different options and ideas. They seem to never be stuck in life. They are highly adaptable. Children developing in the presence of these types of adults routinely grew up into incredible adults themselves, adults who are problem-solvers, not problem creators.

{5.11} One of the better examples of this that I've come across has already happened in several places across our planet. What's going on in the Netherlands is a perfect example of what our species can do when we put our differences aside and work together in a freely open-minded, highly diverse environment.

Multiple times a year, a group of people get together to discuss solutions to the country's current problems. This group of people are from all over the country. The one noticeable difference is the type of people they bring in. All different types of people; different educational backgrounds, different races, different ethnic groups, males, females, different levels of experience, all different areas and levels of knowledge and experience come together for common goals. Goals that will benefit everyone in the country, not just a few people. All with a high degree of common sense and open-mindedness.

They achieved one of the greatest Human achievements of all modern accomplishments. And barely using any of their region of the world to accomplish it. Country-wide benefits to every level of their people. On only 175 acres and 95% chemical free, they have produced enough high quality, life-enhancing, densely nutritious food that not only feeds their entire region of the world, but also allows for a massive income for their countries as well. They are #2 in the world for exporting fruits and vegetables!

Are they a perfect country (region of the world)? No. There's no such thing. But they are one of the more successful modern regions of anywhere else on the planet. They continually adapt their way of life to ease the stresses of their people. They work *with* the Laws of Nature, not *against* them.

*The Laws of Nature have never changed and most likely will not any time soon. Successful people or groups of people understand this. They work with nature, not against it. They adapt to their environment much more than they modify their environment.*

## Examples of Laws of Nature:

*1. Gravity.*

*2. Our gut bacteria, our digestive systems, along with our entire minds, brains, and bodies have been evolving and adapting along with one another along with the Earth and everything else on Earth for several million years.*

*3. Ocean tides.*

*4. High diversity and adaptability are essential to any successful life form.*

*5. The changing seasons.*

*6. The extraordinarily important and essential roles of parenting and teaching life-enhancing skills to their young.*

The big picture was becoming more and more clear to me. Throughout the history of all of us and all other living things, to be successful during our time here is to be highly diversified and highly adaptable to our changing environment.

*If you and I want to have more dynamic control of our lives, then a highly open, highly diversified, and highly adaptable mind is one of the absolute keys to mastering that.*

For example, I went through a painful, stressful career loss that took a big toll on my life. However, I unknowingly stuck myself in a tight, no-way out corner way before I lost my job. This particular career was during the time in my life that I would have defined myself as an "unsuccessful human." I had a good successful career, a few good relationships, good hobbies, good income. I was well respected during my career. But I was close-minded, arrogant, and ignorant. I may have looked good "on paper" but I wasn't made up of the good stuff. I was a superficial, fearful person that depended on others for virtually everything.

As the stress built up during the last couple of years (of that career), it was becoming very apparent to me that a major part of me feeling stuck and hopeless was because of me. I had not built up enough tools, skills, and knowledge to fall back on. I had basically only developed enough skills during my lifetime to hold only two different types of jobs. I had boxed myself in.

Three days after I lost my career, I said this to myself, "To hell with this! I'm not going down like this! I will not let other people control the direction of my life and I will do what I have to do to never be in this position again!" I gave myself three days to bitch, complain, blame, and wallow in my own self-pity. Then I made a plan...

I was going to build and learn as many different skills and abilities as I could over the next few years, so I didn't ever have to depend on others for a paycheck. I never wanted to feel that kind of loss again.

I worked in a wide variety of jobs the few years following (blue collar and white collar jobs). Each offered me a different skill set to be able to use later. Some of these jobs were paying me very low, insulting wages, but I did not care. I had a different purpose this time. I was on a different mission. To become much more independent because I needed and wanted more freedom.

{5.12} A documentary I watched about the Great Depression comes to mind as I write about those tight, restrictive corners we put ourselves in. Those corners continually provide us with very few options.

The first scene shows a large group of happy, seemingly successful, job-holding men who were providing for their families. They were proud. Their life was secure...seemingly.

Then the documentary shows the same men after the Great Depression hits their lives. They then lose their jobs. They lose their security. Within a few days, these once very proud, confident men were not so proud and confident anymore. Many of them were thrown into places they were not *mentally or behaviorally* prepared for.

These large groups of now unemployed adult men were in serious trouble. Few of them ever took the time to develop any useful skills to either find other work or even keep their life together. Many families were destroyed and split under the intense stress.

Can you guess what happened next with these men? Like following yet another Human species script, an all too familiar response to a crisis. Instead of trying to figure out real solutions, they start complaining and blaming. They blamed anything and everyone else for the reasons their lives were falling apart. **To be fair, some of their complaints were warranted.** Many of them did get screwed over when it came to losing their jobs during the Great Depression, so we can't put *all* the blame on them.

However, a few clues about the underlying psyche of our species were exposed during that documentary. It didn't make sense to me either. How could an adult be so happy, proud, confident one day with a job, then become so down, depressed and fearful without a job the next day? Are we that weak of a species?

Apparently. Watching them lose their jobs because of reasons beyond their control was disheartening (of course that is a terrible thing to live through). But watching those same proud men sitting on those dusty sidewalks waiting for something or someone to "save" them was much more disheartening.

We all have the choice to keep learning or to stop learning on our own. It is our decision, no one else's, in which we choose how to build our own brain and mind. We all have the ability to build up our own arsenal of adaptable skills. We don't need good genetics or money to do it either. To me, these men put "all their eggs in one basket." They obviously did not build up any other skills prior to this job and obviously they are still not working to improve themselves sitting on the side of the street feeling sorry for themselves.

They were dependent on others to provide work for them. They were trapped. However, they trapped themselves. They became content with false securities while they stopped learning and acquiring new skills. Their lives and their families' lives became completely dependent on others.

Something else deeply bothered me about these recently unemployed men sitting on the sidewalks. Most of them were family men with kids. First mistake they were making was making it okay to depend on others for work while not working on building any useful skills on their own. Their kids were watching and would most likely follow their father's lead later in life. *What kind of example were they trying to set for their kids anyway?* Secondly, they made it okay to blame others for their problems, instead of seeking out real solutions so this would not happen again to them and their family. They lacked diversity of skills, thoughts and ideas. They had virtually no adaptability. They lacked any kind of long-term vision. They were lacking long-term problem-solving skills. And this is what they chose to pass on to their kids.

*It's important to realize that this scenario plays out every day all over the world in exhausting repetition throughout our species.*

We, our species, still are all these types of people. *I was until I decided I didn't want to be anymore.* One type of Human puts high priority on keeping their job. Although they express how much they need this job, they rarely learn anything more than they need to keep the job. They usually do the least they can do to keep it. They mostly don't see or don't care about developing new or old skills to further themselves. They may even look down and ridicule others who continually work to get better. This is how I was before I decided to change.

On the other hand, successful people take advantage of each new situation as a learning experience, a way to build up their arsenal of skills so they do not become too dependent on any one job or one person or any one group of people. Successful people were most likely not wasting time sitting on the sidewalks feeling bad for themselves while waiting for something or someone to save them. They did not put "all their eggs in one basket." And while on the job, they were continuously working to get better. They don't settle and stop learning because they get a paycheck.

## {5.13} Another One of Our Species' Faults
Our Self-Perceived Self-Image

This Human species' fault, along with the next one we talk about, are heavily intertwined with each other. And if self-image is a species' trait, do other species make decisions based on their own image? Are there other species on Earth that make their life choices based on what their neighbors, friends, or families think of them?

_Human Self-Image_ = *putting the physical image of our Human-selves on a pedestal and continually obsessing over ways to improve how we physically look and physically age while continually ignoring any kind of meaningful development of our Human minds and brains...*

For now, we'll keep our image simple. For this discussion, our image is how we present ourselves to others. Does our presentation to others as ourselves alter our decision making? Do we make most of our decisions based on what we think others will think of us? Do our decisions based on our own perceived self-image affect only our life or does it affect our families, our communities, our cultures, our countries, our species? How deep does this one seemingly harmless trait actually affect us as individuals or as a species?

Before figuring out our species, let's look into the lives of a few other species to see if their image affects their decision making. Remember, virtually all, if not all of our behaviors are found throughout the Animal Kingdom. Animals other than us go through depression, addictions, loss of family members, etc. Do other animals have a self-image? Are they concerned about how they present themselves to others?

Yep, examples are everywhere. We are not close to being the only species that base their decisions on their image. Are we also a species that puts an *unbalanced, high priority* on making important life-decisions based on being accepted by the people around us?

Within and throughout the Animal Kingdom, especially the higher orders of mammals and birds, females of millions of species share a common behavioral trait that has much to do with physical image (what the physical eye perceives only). We find a high degree of using eyes-only judgment of males when the males of a species have little to do with raising the offspring. When we find a species that forms lifelong pair bonds (a single pair of one male and one female forming a lifelong "marriage" to one another where each helps with raising and teaching the young), we find that the females dig a little deeper looking for more than just physical looks in her mate. If she has to spend the rest of her life with one male, he better have much more to offer her than a pretty face.

Most females in most species choose their mates. Males do not choose their mates in most species. Males fight and compete with each other to gain access to the possibility of getting chosen to mate with the female. Many females in many species have evolved over millions of years, selecting the most suitable mate that is also available and nearby. Many females are strikingly picky. If one feather, one hair, one piece of fur is out of place, she may reject him. If she doesn't like the way he dances, the way he flicks his tail, the way he tilts his head, he may lose out. She goes to the next male and analyzes his looks as well as the performance he puts on. Some males in some species do get chosen for favorable behavioral qualities, but many more species make reproductive choices based solely on the external appearance.

Could our species behave like this or have we evolved past that superficial external judgment that many other species possess?

I've been taught my whole life how much better our species is than all other species. It's getting harder and harder to believe that now. I actually think we are becoming one of, if not the worst, species of all time. Of course, we could not be that if we so choose.

Also, just because our species decided to look down upon all other creatures as lower and less complex than us, it doesn't mean they are not performing high levels of complex, adaptable behaviors. Many things are still happening even if we choose not to see them.

There are plenty of examples of lower animals forming...

*1. **Complex Languages** - Whales talking to each other. Several pages of recordings showed how their language included several hundred to possibly a few thousand different sounds (words) that they used to communicate (talk) with one another.*

*2. **High Levels of Parenting** - A mother blue whale picking up her very heavy multi-ton calf out of the water for many, many exhausting hours in an attempt to protect it from a never-ending killer whale attack.*

*3. **Building Complex Structures** - Ant hills. Ants build complex mounds with perfect ventilation to bring in fresh air with oxygen while removing toxic air with built-up carbon dioxide.*

*4. **Learning/Analyzing** - This is constantly found in predator-prey relationships. Each is always trying to out-evolve the other by observing, learning, analyzing, and then adapting.*

*5. **Planning/Executing** - A pack of wolves planning a group attack on a herd of elk. The pack of wolves comes up with a plan, shares it with the other members, then carries it out. Each wolf has their own set of instructions and path to take to carry out the attack.*

We have many of our own species who can barely do any of these. How can other animals learn these complex behaviors and pass them on to their offspring while our species struggles to learn and pass beneficial behaviors to our own offspring?

*We are supposed to be the species that has finally evolved to the point that we can dominate these and many other animalistic behaviors.*

What does this all have to do with image? We'll get there. Back to choosy females for a bit. Being exceptionally choosy when selecting a mate based solely on the perfection of the external physique may be very beneficial for many species, but it does not mean it's beneficial for ours. This is one of those traits that can rip a species like ours apart. A weak-minded species will have a very hard time existing with this type of behavior.

Some of our natural animalistic behaviors should be further groomed and sharpened for use while some behaviors are an insult to our species and should be minimized to nearly nothing. This one is one of those. It makes zero sense, especially with all our species has accomplished, that we are still judging each other solely based on what we look like, how we dress, how much money we make, and what kind of fancy, prestigious job we or our family may have.

**Highly disappointing trait for an advanced species to possess!**

Successful, confident, badass individuals, families, neighborhoods, cities, and cultures have long been done with this superficial, time-wasting, lower animal-like behavior. It puts too many limits on their life. They do not like unnecessary limits that inhibit their growth. Successful Humans are really good with superficial things like money and their physical image *(they are usually both financially stable and physically fit and healthy)*; however, they rarely allow them to become an unbalanced dominant force in their life.

{5.14} This next example of how self-image is highly intertwined in our decision-making occurs during the North American Civil War. The story goes like this. The Southern Confederate Army against the Northern Union Army. At this stage of the war, the South was outgunned and outmanned. They were also lacking the sophistication of weapons the North had. However, they were not ready to give up.

Then the Union Army started building a variety of different cannons. These cannons had different shot patterns than the older, more commonly used cannons. Instead of shooting one big lead projectile, which is mostly what made-up the South's cannons; they were able to shoot wider patterns of smaller projectiles, creating a new weapon essentially. The North basically turned some of their cannons into very large shotguns. But those individual "pellets" were no joke. They were a solid mass of perfectly rounded balls of lead one inch in diameter. Hundreds of them would exit the cannon with each shot. Those cannons caused serious damage to anything in its way.

Back at the battlefield, the Confederate Army was marching toward the Union Army. Confederate soldiers started to debate with one another if it's a good idea to continue walking toward these cannons. A few of them mentioned they could just turn around and go home. They did not have to walk toward their own death. Then others decided to shout their opinion, "Anyone who chooses to go home will forever be labeled a coward by your friends, families, and neighbors! If you are not a coward, keep walking toward the Union soldiers!"

The vast majority of them walked right into their deaths as the 1-inch solid lead pellets ripped and shredded large chunks of their bodies. So many of those soldiers chose death over their own self-preservation. They chose to die a horrendous death because they were worried about what their friends, families, and neighbors thought about them. And some of these men were fathers. That is all-time selfish and incredibly stupid Human behavior.

Does our image really mean that much that we care more about what others think about us rather than making logical, common sense decisions? That was just one example and this is definitely not just found in the Southern part of the United States. This is Human behavior. Most of us deal with this destructive behavior all day every day.

*Are my life and decisions based on what others will think of me too? I wondered how many of my daily decisions were based on what others thought about it.*

Personally, this was one of my worst traits that I possessed. I think over 90% of who I was and what I did was built around what I thought others would think about it. I was weak, I wanted to fit in, and I wanted to be accepted. So, I continually gave in.

How I dressed, how I acted, what I watched on TV, the music I listened to, was all superficially chosen so other people around me would think I was cool and not a loser. I didn't even like most of what I was doing but the importance of my self-perceived image toward others was so much more important than anything else. It makes me sick to my stomach to think of all the wasted time I have spent on this Earth trying to be a certain way so the people around me "may" like me. I lost my life. My life was for everybody else, not me. I didn't even know what I liked. I didn't even know what kind of person I was. I just continually followed the mainstream.

{5.15} I began to add up people in my life; the ones I was seemingly molding and creating my entire life around or for. If I put so much emphasis on what my friends, family, and neighbors thought of me and my life, then I needed to see how it played out over a larger scale. I counted the average number of people I may come into "contact" with every day (eye contact, talking to, or close enough contact where we are able to see each other's physical appearance). Depending on the size of the city you live in, you may only have contact with a handful of people a day to a few hundred to several thousand.

If I divided the number of people I came into contact with every day by (/) our species population (~ 8 billion=8,000,000,000) then times (X) that by 100, then I could see what the percentage was of our species that I was prioritizing most of my life choices on.

I would typically come into "contact" with about 300 people (including family and close friends) every day.

300/8,000,000,000 = 0.0000000375 (100) = 0.00000375%.

I was molding and creating my life, my mind, my brain for that percentage of our species, 0.00000375%! What a huge waste of time it was for me to waste on trying to get others around me to like or accept me.

What if I was really popular and I was exposed to 30,000 (including family and close friends) people every day. Then I should definitely make my decisions based on that many people, right? Well...30,000/8 billion = **0.000375%.** I'm still not even close to just 1% of our entire species. Let's add social media to our contact list. I'm hypothetically up to 30 million contacts every day which would = 0.375% of our total species. Closer but still not there.

*I would need 80 million "friends" or "contacts" to add up to just 1% of our entire species.*

Why the hell would I base and prioritize my personal life decisions for my life on such a low percentage of our species and their personal opinions?

That quote, "What will the neighbors think?" brought a whole new meaning to me. A different, darker meaning that could rip families apart, rip communities apart, rip relationships apart... I became disgusted with myself and what I was becoming; what I allowed myself to become. This debilitating species trait had undoubtedly spawned a vicious, yet highly sneaky grasp on so many areas of my life. Although previously mentioned, I'll comment here on the high importance of self-confidence and self-worth. If I had any self-worth or confidence, I would make my life decisions based on common sense, intellect, and long-term vision, not because of what people might think of me and my decisions.

*Successful Humans carry around high levels of self-worth and inner confidence. They make informed, intellectual, common sense decisions that may not follow what the "crowd" is doing. They realize that spending time obsessing over their own self-image is highly overrated and mostly a huge waste of time. They work tirelessly on inner growth, not trying to be accepted by others. Interestingly enough, they are usually quite attractive since they continually work on their inner self!*

Our species' obsession with self-image penetrates and invades the tiniest corners of our lives. If we are not careful, it will take us over little by little. Especially when it comes to the children around us who we are responsible for. When our perceived importance of our own self-image begins and stays, problems will always follow.

*Some of our darkest qualities of our species hide right here. There are zero relationships in our species as important as that between parents and their children or guardian or mentor and child. Adults of our species, most species really, are responsible for developing their young while teaching them as many usable skills as possible, which in turn would make their lives easier and more manageable as they get older.*

*Also, if we teach them correctly, they become much less dependent on us the older they get.*

I noticed this regrettable trait in myself first. I continually put my needs before the kids around me. My stuff was always more important than theirs. I thought my friends wouldn't think I was cool if I played with or gave attention to the kids. Unfortunately, for too many situations, I was right. Many adults did think I was a loser if I was playing and interacting with kids. But maybe I was the real loser. I was more worried about what the adults thought of me rather than doing what was the right and best thing for the kids.

I was completely disgusted with myself. I was a shallow, spineless adult who just followed the crowd. This couldn't be right. I had to find another way to live. I was not comfortable with this path of life. I could not go through life making decisions based on fear of rejection anymore.

As I played out the scenario of me shedding my image and possibly appearing "uncool" or "unpopular" in front of a group of adults in my head, I realized it was going to be exceptionally difficult. I needed much more confidence to pull that off. The thought of being ridiculed, mocked, isolated, hated, or rejected did not appeal to me at first. Deep in my brain, the fear of rejection was overpowering and overwhelming to me. I couldn't believe how weak I was. On paper and to many people in my life, I was believed to be successful. Then why was it so hard to stand up to the adults around me who looked down on me? I was a coward. It was much easier to abandon a child's needs than it was to stand up to a group of adults. That same group of adults who made up an exceptionally small percentage of our species.

But I just had to find out. I had to find out what it felt like to disregard the opinionated opinions of the small-minded adults around me. I slowly but surely built up my own self-confidence...little by little. I explain how I did this in *Chapter 3*. It was quite challenging to stand against and opposite to the ones I was always standing next to. However, after everything was said and done, the highs completely suffocated the lows during this experience.

*I built up my self-worth and inner confidence "behind the scenes" and when the time was right, I broke away. I broke away from everyone telling me who to be and how to live. I was free of their cynical control over me...*

*And every time thereafter, I found it to be much more enjoyable to hang out with the young ones...*

{5.16} Before we go into the next fault of our species, let's go a little deeper into the subtle undertone that was present in the last section. The undertone was that I was feeling that something was off...really off. I was feeling something deeper than superficial feelings. I wasn't sure what to do with them or what they were. I was taught different ways to deal or not to deal with feelings and emotions. I was taught by females around me that it was okay to have emotions and feelings. However, I was mostly taught that having emotions or feelings makes you look weak (mostly by the male adults in my life). You look like a "less-than" and "weak," I was told.

What's the point of feelings and emotions anyway? Are they really that important? Can I maximize my potential as a Human if I don't deal with them? Do other species have feelings and emotions? Why do some people ignore them while others are way too deep into them? Should we "master" these as well? Is it beneficial in the long run to ignore them or is it better to deal with them in the opposite way, head-on?

My thoughts went straight to lions on a savannah. As a lion approaches a savannah, she doesn't automatically start running around hoping to randomly run by a prey animal that just happens to be injured, slow, or weak. She waits and watches. She is unbiasedly observing and learning before she makes her move... What is she looking for?

A weak link. A weak link that she can exploit. But how can she figure out which one is the weak link? It's not like she can talk to them..

But is the lioness only using her external senses to identify prey or is she using something deep inside of her? A feeling deep inside her. A feeling that supplements those external senses (hearing, smelling, seeing, touching). A feeling that allows her to pinpoint the weakest of the weak. It's virtually the same feeling we get when we walk into a room full of people that we don't know. Before words are even spoken, we tend to migrate toward the people we "feel" comfortable with and move away from the people we don't "feel" comfortable with. Why? How? We're not talking. How do we know who to be comfortable and safe with to stand or sit by? Like every living thing that has ever existed, we all have the ability to be able to assess our environment for safety or danger. Most of this is done without verbal communication.

Then there must be something beneath external senses that allows living things to be able to "read a room." What are we made up of then? Cells. Cells that are made up of very small parts called molecules (like proteins, fats, carbohydrates that we eat), which are made up of atoms (like sodium, chlorine, or hydrogen), which are made up of subatomic particles (neutrons, electrons, protons). The point to all of this is hidden within what holds these subatomic particles together. It's simple. Energy! And when it comes down to that deep-down energy that controls everything about us and our world, there are only three ways for them to respond and behave...

*1. They move <u>toward</u> one another because they are attracted to each other. (positive energy)*

*2. They move <u>away</u> from each other because they repel each other. (negative energy)*

*3. They do not move, or they move from side to side and stay <u>equal</u> distance from one another. (neutral energy)*

Think of a magnet. There is something that is invisible that can repel the *non-attracted* sides of it with tremendous force. Nothing natural can push them together. Same as when they are *attracted to* each other; they're very hard to pull apart. Of course, in living systems, there is variation in how much force is used to keep molecules and atoms together. Some molecules can be separated easily while others are nearly impossible to separate.

Everything that enters our bodies, heads (brains), or minds has either one of those three fundamental responses. Some are attracted to our cells and can <u>enhance</u> them, some are repelled by them and may <u>harm</u> them, some are <u>neutral</u> and have no reaction. The closer we match our environment to what our cells are attracted to, formed relationships with, and have evolved with for millions of years, the better performing all our cells become.

*As with everything else in the living world, there are exceptions to the "rules." Some cells that are attracted to each other can cause harm while others that are rejected can be beneficial. Also, some of our cells, like our disease-fighting white blood cells, are intentionally attracted to non-recognized foreign cells, so as to dispose of them. But for the most part, most cells, molecules, and other micro-structures in our bodies respond in one of the three ways talked about previously.*

{5.17} So, it's pretty fair to say that there is some kind of energy that flows within us and between us and between all living things. We can label it whatever we want, but if there is an underlying energy that controls the deepest parts of us, it would no doubt permeate into every other part of anything that is living. So, if energy drives us and all other life and it's everywhere around us, why do so many adults in our species continue to diminish the importance of energy "feelings" between us?

Maybe because it's too hard to control. Many of us, way too many of us in our species, are driven by power and control. It's hard to have power over something that you can't control. For the adults of our species, dealing with one's feelings and emotions or their "energy" is seen as beneath them. Many adults think that anyone that deals with any kind of Human emotion, feeling or energy is weak.

*It may be hard for many of us to deal with, but right behind the fear of not dealing with them is where we find many of the answers to who we are and what we are truly made up of. And the Humans we have to live with on this planet that reject or downplay the importance of this highly important Human trait, will try to persuade us otherwise.*

### To control what can't be controlled by others is powerful.

When you and I have dominant control over our own emotions, feelings, and energy, it destroys the control others have over them. I control my own emotions and feelings, not other people. I know they can make me or break me. I choose for them to make me. I will not hide from them anymore...

*I choose to keep them closer rather than unreachable.*

My *control* over my feelings and emotions are like prized weapons, always there when I need them. And the more I use them, the better I get at using them. Using love and empathy as the answer for every one of my problems was not the answer, just as using anger and jealousy to solve every one of my problems wasn't either. Neither way was diversified or adaptable enough. Then the use of negative energy-filled emotions like anger and jealousy took me down even further. Be very wary of negative-energy emotions (like hate, greed, pride, judgment, anger, jealousy, etc). They can bring long-term chaos into your life while NOT showing any short-term signs of negativity.

I also realized it took way more strength to recognize and deal with my feelings and emotions than to not deal with them. Whichever adults have ever believed that dealing with our inner feelings makes us weak, were very, very wrong! Just because they were too weak to face their true emotions and feelings, doesn't mean that you and I have to be.

Allowing myself to be normal and confront my feelings and emotions rather than run away from them proved to be monumental in the long run!

**A large portion of achieving personal inner strength and personal freedom is being able to deal with and handle a variety of emotions and feelings as they arise.**

And for the first time in my life, I was in control of my reactions to life's challenges. Also, once I became open to learning about and controlling my emotions, my lows in my life became less and less. My lows, when I did get them, didn't keep me down for long. Also, my recovery time from being down was starting to pick up pace.

## {5.18} Yet Another One of Our Species' Faults:
Telling Others What to do

As I studied and observed our species over the years, another not-so-good trait kept showing itself. This trait continually showed up in individuals, families, cities, cultures, etc. throughout our species.

This potentially toxic, disruptive trait was an easy one to miss. I overlooked it for a while. Then once I noticed it, it became overbearing. It was everywhere. And yet again, it was rarely found in successful Humans. Over and over, many of us would do it... I sure did.

Our species has a seriously frustrating problem with telling others what to do, who to be, and how to live. Some of us are constantly barking out orders and opinions on how we should do this that way and do that this way. Live like this, live like that... Believe this but not that... Be this type of person, be that type of person... Do this career, do that career. Constant and exhausting rules and directions for who to be and how to live life coming from adults who have no business telling others what to do.

Guess what the successful Humans did with this toxic trait? They don't use it. They allowed others around them, of all ages, to make their own decisions and their own mistakes. They talked about what they did during those similar life situations, but they did not guide, lie, manipulate, or steer them where they thought they should go.

*We can be an exhausting species with all of our made up man-made rules and instructions on how to live and who to be. I guess it makes many of us feel safe when we have so many man-made laws and rules, but to others, it's quite suffocating.*

{5.19} Too many of us in our species are obsessed with power and control. It's pretty easy to point out the individuals among us that can become highly toxic with their inability to control their unhealthy obsession with power and control. The waves of chaos and destruction that seem to always follow them fall into a spectrum of variation like many things. Some people who have an unhealthy obsession with power and control were barely noticeable while others were highly noticeable. All types are everywhere. They are not rare within our species. Once someone gets a little control or power over someone else (like a boss over an employee, parent over a child, or an elected official over a group of people, etc), this can begin to overtake them. It can overtake any type of common sense, long-term, intelligent decision making. Most of us can be taken down this dark path when we are given a little power or a little control over someone else. We waste an incredible amount of our time here as an advanced species trying to control the lives of others.

*This is a major flaw of our species that should be dealt with head-on if one wishes to rise to the level of being a highly successful Human Being.*

Wherever there is a hint of something or someone that can be controlled or manipulated, you can bet that some of the worst types of our species will not be far behind. But again, it isn't just these selfish, narcissistic people who are the problem. It's many more of us than just them. Most of us Humans can be built into these types of people depending on the developmental environment we grew up in. In my opinion, the majority of selfish, narcissistic, sociopathic, psychopathic people are made, not born. We, as a species, make them, over and over again...

This type of toxic Human trait is so easy to fall into, even for the most secure person. We, myself included, think that we are helping someone by telling them what to do and how to do it, but in reality, we could be hurting our relationship with that person without noticing. I think it is so deeply buried in our Human DNA *(this trait is almost non-existent in all other species)* that it is quite natural to fall back into for virtually all of us.

It's our deep, deep, deep need that most of us, most of our species, have; the need to feel above other people. The need to feel like we are better than the people around us. If we don't pay attention to this damaging trait, it will pull us in. It will pull us deeper and deeper into it. This can be a very dark Human path to take.

Look at the following lines and the relationship between them.
(Line A-B) (Line C-D)

### Relationship Example 1:

Line A --------------------        Line B ----—------------------

### Relationship Example 2:

*Line C* --------------------

       Line D _____

I can make an argument that this simplistic line analogy above can either destroy or enhance every single relationship in our life. Line A and Line B can represent any type of relationship we have with another person. Line A can be a parent while Line B being the child. Line A can be a boyfriend while Line B can be the girlfriend. Line A can be the husband while line B can be the wife. Line A could be a boss while Line B could be an employee.

*Before we move into that, let's clear something up first. Of course, we need laws and rules to govern our families and cities but there is a sweet spot where laws and rules enhance our lives. If we exceed that sweet spot with too many unnecessary rules and laws, whether within families, cities, cultures, or countries, we GUARANTEE ourselves constant problems. Too many unnecessary rules and laws in our homes, cities, and schools are once again taking away people's personal freedom to make their own choices and to make their own mistakes.*

*Lack of personal freedom nearly always leads to the worst of Human behaviors.*

In simplicity, the relationship between Line A (person A) and Line B (person B) are equal and healthy. The relationship between Line C (person C) and Line D (person D) are unequal and unhealthy. Person C looks down upon person D, doesn't respect them, and does not think they are equal to them.

With regards to the relationship between Line (person) C and Line (person) D, our species is infested with this toxic, species-destroying trait. Families are some of the worst culprits of this. So many of us seem to be in constant search of trying to control other people's lives. Why? What is wrong with us?

With that in mind, I find it fascinating how much time we (I) spend (waste) on other people's lives. That's exactly how I was for most of my life. I followed the lives of others. I knew more about the lives of celebrities and neighbors down the road than I did my own life. I was also heavily invested in the life decisions of the people around me. If someone made a decision about their own life that I did not agree with, I made it known, and argued with them that they are making the wrong decision for their *own* life. Just writing that out made me laugh. What an incredible waste of life that is; to worry so much about what others think, believe, and do. And I was doing it all the time! Worrying way more about other people's lives than my own. It was so much easier to deal with their issues than my own.

I would tell people what they should do even if I didn't completely understand the advice I was giving them. But it sure felt good telling people what they should do with their life. However, it did come my way too. I was only giving advice to people who I perceived to be beneath me, unequal to me.

There were way more people "above" me than "below" me with me being the sensitive, insecure, low self-worth type. I was told who to be, how to live, and how to think very often. And when I stood up to the people who were butting into my life, the same old boring, lame response so many of us will naturally go to (I as well). I was mocked, ridiculed, belittled, and labeled. They would never ever let me rise to their level (Line). That's where many fights or heated discussions started. They would never, ever let me, no matter the costs, rise to their level. In their eyes, I would always be beneath them. Any threat to that would be immediately and sometimes viciously rebuked.

I did it too. I'm no different. I have the same species flaws we all have. As soon as I got a little edge or power over others, I fell into the same groove many of us do; telling others what to do and disregarding what they thought or felt about it. If they tried to challenge me, my ideas, or rules, I went to an all too familiar go-to. I hid behind the rules and laws of whatever position I was in. Instead of trying to work with others and seeing them as equals, I decided power and unbalanced inequality was the better way to go. It always, always, always eventually crashed and burned.

{5.20} What's the point? What's the point in telling others what to do and who to be? Is that really our purpose? To continually invade other people's lives? To control and impress our power over them? It can't be. What a terrible way to live. A complete waste of time in most situations for our advanced species.

Just listen to us. We are constantly telling each other how to eat, what to eat, what career we should have, what to wear, how to speak, how to think, who or what to believe in, and the list goes on and on and on. Too many of us within our species think we should be making personal life decisions for others. It is one of our most disgusting, disturbing, inhibiting, and life-sucking traits we have. We try to control everything and everyone around us. That damn square-peg-round-hole analogy again.

*We (Humans) are in constant need of forcing our "square" ideas and beliefs into others' "round" ideas and beliefs.*

Eventually you and I and whoever else wants to get out of this species-derived mess we're in will start to deeply understand that all of these faulty traits we all possess are heavily intertwined and connected with one another. One bad trait feeds the next one and so on. However, if these species traits are interconnected and feed off one another, many can fall if one or two are fixed.

That's why the most successful Humans in the history of our planet are continually really good at real, true, core Human traits; the fundamental traits that won't allow the toxic traits to take hold of them or their family. High self-worth, self-built inner confidence, open-mindedness, diversity, and adaptability of mind are the traits that dominate who they are. Those toxic species' traits that hold so many of us back are beneath them and wasteful. They do not waste time telling others how to live or who to be. They believe in letting people make their own decisions, make their own mistakes, and hopefully learn from them.

Highly successful Humans mostly believe it's a waste of time to help people who never help themselves. However, they will spend an enormous amount of their own time helping others who really want to get better but are struggling in life.

If someone you are trying to help continually makes the same mistakes over and over without trying anything different, it is mostly pointless for you to waste time helping them. If someone refuses to try new ideas or new ways of doing something, that is perfectly okay, but it is their own choice and their own fault, no one else's. And they should take responsibility for what happens, no one else. How could I *not* blame myself if I continually end up in the same place by making the same choices?

For example, there have been several people dying over the last few years due to falling off the sides of cliffs in National Parks. They were falling off the side of cliffs because they were trying to take selfies (pictures of themselves). At this point in Human history, most of us know that it's dangerous to be close to the edge of a cliff. If one chooses to hang off the side of a cliff to take pictures of themselves, all responsibility should fall onto that individual.

Of course the normal reaction is to put blame on the National Park. They are responsible for the safety of their customers, right?

Well yes, but to a point. You can't protect against stupidity. It doesn't matter how many signs, railings, laws or safety measures you put in place, there will always be stupid. We cannot protect everyone from everything. We all get one life. It is up to each of us to protect our own selves from our own decisions. That's not the job for everyone else.

Most of us have access now to basically the same information. We are living during the Information Era of our species. We all have the right and the ability to consume all the information out there the way we want to. If we personally choose to stop learning and building our own brains to maximize our own intelligence, that is on us, nobody else.

Take our Human diets for example. We dig much deeper into this in *Chapter 3,* so I'll keep it to a minimum here as it relates to the point of letting people make their own choices. It's eerily similar to the previous example of letting people take dangerous selfies if they want. If the person died because of neglect by the National Park, that's different and not what we're talking about here. However, most of us should understand the risk of standing next to the edge of a cliff, guard rails or not. When someone decides to put their own life at risk for something that they chose to do, that is their absolute right. If they die doing it, they chose to put their own life in that position, nobody else. When things like this happen, why do so many of us rush to fix or solve it? I know that's my first reaction.

*Sometimes we can't solve stupid. We spend and waste too much of our time, as a species, trying to save stupid.*

To me, the human diet and our view of it is much like that. There is an immense amount of information about how and what we should and should not eat. It can become overwhelming with all the data, much of which contradicts itself. It can become incredibly difficult to figure out how to eat in a way that allows us to remain sane and relatively healthy. (We figured that out in Chapter 3). We have plenty of information to make common sense decisions on what I want to eat and how that fits into the person I want to become. Not everybody wants to live a long life, so their diet would correspond to that, as would a diet for someone who wanted to live a long life.

By now, and during this time of our species' existence, most of us adults should have a reasonably good idea of what to eat to lengthen our life or what to eat that would shorten it. Once we become adults, we have every right to eat whatever we want whenever we want. It gets tiresome and annoying when we tell each other what our diet should be. Your diet should never be a concern of mine as my diet should never be a concern of yours, unless we are equally sharing ideas of course.

Most of us realize by now that we have a chance of dying earlier than we should if we dominate our diets with certain types of foods for long periods of time. We are "sitting on the edge of a cliff." At any time after years and years of self-abuse and neglect to our own bodies, we can "slip and fall off of the edge of the cliff." A sudden cardio (heart) event may occur. Stroke, heart attack, ruptured aneurysm, etc. happens. We slip off the edge of the cliff. We die way earlier than we should. As callous as this sounds, why should we care? It's their life and they made their own decisions for their health based on how they viewed life. The person who died taking a selfie on a cliff is just as aware of the dangers as a person living today knowing the real possibility of an early death that a less than healthy diet will bring.

We are all capable of making our own decisions. It's nobody else's business what you or I put into our bodies. I will *benefit* or *suffer* from my own decisions and mine only. The rest of us should respect that.

*Our species cannot "fix" everything and everyone. Our species would benefit greatly by getting the hell out of the way by allowing people to suffer or flourish from their own decisions.*

{5.21} Let's go back to where we left off in section 5.19 when we were talking about the Lines of Relationships. In some parts of some relationships, some unequalness is required. Many relationships may be able to exist, but definitely not thrive with inequality embedded within it. A boss has the right, as is the nature of the job role, to be above the employee when it comes to the job. Line A moves above Line B. They are not equal anymore per the job description. The boss (Line A) moves above employee (Line B). But in every other scenario in life as a Human dealing with Human rights, Line B is equal to Line A. Line A may not believe that or like it or accept it, but it does not matter what Line A thinks. **Line A and Line B will always be equal because they are both Human and possess the same Human rights!**

*We all came from the same place, we are all one in the same species, we all deserve the same Rights.*

What would our species become if we were able to overcome and conquer this shameful, archaic animalistic behavior and obsession of always having to be above others? We are woefully bad at working equally with others who are different from us. **We would be an unstoppable advanced species if we could get past this one enormous flaw.** If we worked with each other, especially those of us who look and believe differently than ourselves, instead of constantly fighting with each other over petty differences, we would be able to accomplish and fix almost every problem we have right now as a species.

Our species, when compared to the entire history of our planet, is a young, juvenile species. And we continually express that age and the problems that come with juvenile decisions. We have all the information, knowledge, technology, and intellect to solve any problem that we currently face. But we are far from being able to put it all together because of our current mental state.

*I have built up this undeniable, deeply anxious type of feeling deep down when I think about how this one simple concept can rip a species apart. It did not matter where I looked, where there was inequality in relationships, there was the worst of our species. Where I found equality in relationships, I found the very best that our species had to offer.*

We fail miserably at this concept throughout our short history here. So many of us revolve our life and almost every decision about our life on our "Line" being higher than the others around us. Our entire existence seems to revolve around being better than the "others." Even if it negatively impacts our families or even our own life. Throughout history, so many of us have chosen these same paths.

In modern times, you can see this everywhere, every day, every place you look, especially in the business, for-profit world. Climbing the company ladder, no matter the cost, even if it hurts myself and my family in the long run, comes to mind. Why? Why do so many of our species continue to fall into this fault? Maybe it's so we can think of ourselves as greater than another group of people. How many times have we neglected our own kids to gain a little bit of power, a little bit of "I'm better (above) than someone else?"

### _The Universe's most powerful addiction?_

_Thinking that my thoughts, beliefs, ideas, way of life, is better than yours. When I look-down, ridicule, mock, or hate another person or group of people I instantly feel better about myself, even if it lasts for a short time. When I am not happy with my life or I'm in a low I'll start blaming and complaining about others. I instantly feel better in the short term. When I get angry or frustrated with life, I take a "hit" of inequality and start hating and blaming others who are different than me. This "hit" of inequality can eventually become a full-on addiction where we will have to take many "hits" of hate every day. This addiction, like other addictions, can destroy everything in its path._

So, at this point, I don't give a shit anymore about what Human adults say about emotions and feelings not being important and not being able to be taught and controlled. No matter what others say, we have the ability to benefit greatly from the use of our feelings and emotions.

*Developing feelings and emotions can absolutely be taught and learned unless they genetically can't (which is very rare). The environment in which the child's brain develops is immensely more important than the genes inherited from their parents.*

Those of us born with the capability of feeling, which is most of us, have the ability to learn empathy toward other Humans. We are born with the capabilities of looking at another as an equal, no matter who. Young kids don't care what race another kid is, or what kind of clothes they wear, or how much money their parents have. They are making decisions based on if they feel comfortable with them. They are feeling their environment out. If another kid has good, fun energy, no matter what they look like, they will most likely hang out together. Kids* nearly always see other kids as equals. They don't care who is above who. What happens to that way of living as they become adults? Most of us adults started off as kids who were fully accepting of others who were different. What is happening to us as adults?

*\* Of course, some kids will try to dominate and control other kids around them and treat them as unequal, but mostly it is not as toxic as when adults engage in this type of behavior.*

{5.22} I've come to realize that we are a species in constant conflict. From book clubs to hunting clubs, no matter where we look, adults engage in conflict with each other. I believe a very small portion of that is genetically controlled. I believe a much larger portion responsible for the conflicts within our species is not genetically programmed into us, it's learned, and dependent on our surroundings during our childhood development years. It's not the kids of our species that are engaged in constant conflicts, it's us adults. We are all the problems of our species. It can't be the kids; they learn everything from us adults. We teach them everything, directly and indirectly.

*Everywhere and every time throughout the history of our species where we find inequality or the lack of personal freedom, we find conflicts... Always and forever.*

Doesn't matter where I looked, even inside of us. When I restricted personal freedom by becoming close-minded and rigid, constant internal conflict ensued in my own head. Even in cultures that restricted different ideas, conflicts were constant. Families, cities, countries, it did not matter, same behavior, same results. Over and over again, same Human behaviors, same Human conflicts. History on repeat...

*Inequality = Conflicts*
*Loss of Personal Freedom = Conflicts*

{5.23} What can we personally do about all this conflict? As disheartening as it can become, reflecting on our species-debilitating faults, it's also quite enlightening to realize the incredibly powerful problem-solving traits we possess. Some of the best advice I ever received stands up here, "Clean up your side of the street first." Even if our lives slip into chaos or conflict or any kind of stress, we can still personally stay afloat above it all. We can do it by consistently maintaining our side of the street, by consistently developing an open-minded, highly diversified and highly adaptable, problem-solving brain. By doing this ourselves and for ourselves, we will continue to dodge the patterned, predictable pitfalls of life that the majority of our species continue to fall into. And when we do fall on challenging, stressful times, our drop won't be as far down as it used to be. Our recovery time to all stressors (internal and external) will quicken. Our times of feeling low, depressed, or down on life will become less and less.

*When we become more dependent on ourselves, we become less dependent on others. When we become less dependent on others, they begin to lose their control over us as we become more and more free.*

Think about the recovery time it takes communities to recover from a natural disaster. Who do we think will recover the fastest? Community A, who took time throughout their life to better themselves, continually learn as well as becoming more independent rather than dependent on others for help. Or Community B who decided not to learn new skills and chose to become dependent on others for their livelihoods. The more we are dependent on others, the less we are. Community B could be waiting for a very long time for someone to help them rebuild their lives and homes while Community A had the confidence and the skills to start building right away, not having to wait for others. That's power and freedom!

{5.24} To become an independent and free-minded Human, it helps to know what we are up against and the types of people that we will encounter throughout life. Understanding the patterns of certain types of people can help us avoid a lot of wasted time and energy. And those are two of the most precious parts of life. We all have a limited amount of time and a limited amount of energy while on this planet. Why waste it on certain types of people?

There is a type of us (whether genetically born this way or environmentally developed this way) that only cares about themselves and only cares about their image of being greater than everyone else.

This Human trait is more toxic than money or possessions. It's the unhealthy obsession of seeing others as less than you. No matter what, this type of person will do anything to keep their "Line" above ours. They will lie, cheat, steal, abandon or neglect kids, abandon or neglect spouses, manipulate, alter facts, abuse, and use anybody in their way. In their eyes, we can never be equal to them, ever!

We are now getting into some of the most toxic Human mentalities throughout our history. These toxic, chaos-creating, me-only type mentalities are found throughout our entire species. They are usually all around us. They are our wives, husbands, our brothers and sisters, our bosses, church leaders, hospital and school administrators, managers, etc, etc, etc. They are everywhere and most are not born like this, most are made.

The places that were the most suitable for the growing and developing of these types of mentalities were becoming easier to spot. Not too hard to guess which types of communities would produce more emotionally detached, selfish people. Close-minded, unadaptable, unaccepting, personal-freedom restricting communities are breeding grounds for the self-absorbed narcissistic type of mentality. Throw in some lack of accountability and some good ol' inequality and we have the perfect ingredients to create many more of these types of personalities.

These types of mentalities continually look for people or places to manipulate and exploit. They probe for weaknesses. They want to feel good about themselves and they do not like being challenged. They prey upon the weak, the fearful or the downtrodden. They rarely waste time on the most successful Humans among us. They like easy wins.

There will always be some of our species that disregards humanity, integrity, and common sense for their own personal gain all the while causing waves of chaos wherever they go. However, they have weaknesses, just like we all do. They tend to avoid people with high self-esteem, high self-confidence, and high self-worth. Although these types of people are nothing like a lion, because most of them are cowards, we can still use the following analogy. When a lion *(or most living things, really)* approaches the Savannah *(or anywhere)* looking for their next meal, they first look for weaknesses. Weaknesses that they can exploit. Too much wasted time and energy trying to overcome a confident, strong antelope (or any other living thing). Much easier to dominate, control, and eventually destroy the weakest, least confident antelope (i.e. person). They'll even choose the antelope (person) that has the least amount of options for escaping. It's easier to control and dominate an antelope with one escape route option versus one with many options.

*Maybe this is why many serial killers target victims that have very few options and are considered as being vulnerable individuals, like prostitutes working on the street. So many murderers have watched, observed, and learned which of their potential victims would be the easiest to overcome. So many of them chose the lowest of the low. They chose the victims that would offer the least resistance.*

As much as I think labeling others is restrictive and close-minded, I will put a broad label on this type of behavior. For me, it was important to realize that these types of mentalities were not in some faraway place, but all around me. Also—and this is of utmost importance to our species so it's worth repeating— we, as a species, create most of these types of people. They are not all born like this. We, as a species, are to blame for many of these types. The selfish, me-first and me-only types of personalities. They range from the psychopathic or sociopathic and the narcissistic to the selfish. They believe their needs, beliefs, ideas, and desires are more important than anyone else's. They believe their needs, beliefs, ideas, and desires are more important than even the planet itself.

For the most part, they all have some similarities and follow some of the same basic patterns:

--> *Your needs are always less important than theirs.*

--> *Reasoning with them using your emotions and feelings are discounted, ridiculed, and ignored.*

--> *They seem to be great people and great family members, publicly on the surface, anyway. Behind closed doors, it's a different story. They are the first to abandon, neglect, or abuse their spouses, their own kids, coworkers, employees, etc.*

--> *They will tell their kids how much they love them while barely spending any useful, quality time with them.*

--> *Outwardly appearances are exceptionally important to them.*

--> *Truth and integrity are viewed as weaknesses.*

--> *They think most people are beneath them.*

--> *It's essential that they are liked by the public.*

I would no longer be the weak, "easy-to-take-advantage-of" antelope anymore. I would no longer offer them the weakness they were searching for, waiting to pounce on and overtake. One of the most powerful examples of this I ever came across is a small city in a high state of violence. Continual raping, torturing, and killing of innocent people, even on the streets during the middle of the day.

{5.25} As I was writing this book I was continually looking in as many different areas that I could within our species to see if I could pick up patterns of behavior. I observed and learned. Observed, learned, and connected. Over and over in as many corners of our species that I could, I observed and learned from the people and cultures and beliefs that were different from mine. I opened up and allowed my brain and mind to start connecting dots with all this new, different information.

While observing and learning about different places and different cultures, I came across a video about a city that was in the middle of a very violent time period. As I was watching the video, I incorrectly assumed that what I was watching occurred a very long time ago and did not pertain to life today. Nope, it was happening now. Maybe it was making me feel more comfortable that this kind of inhumane disturbing violence couldn't be happening now. It had to be a long time ago, right? Oh no, it was happening now and most likely, still is.

The city was controlled by a group of individuals with a massive amount of power and untouchability. As familiar as this age-old story goes, they controlled the police and the government. They did as they wanted when they wanted. This group would frequently visit this particular part of town where the poverty rate was very high. There were more women and children than men who lived there as well. This part of town was disregarded and looked down upon as less than Human. They were treated as such. Over and over and over this group of powerfully corrupt men would harass, assault (sexually and physically), rape, and murder whoever they wanted, whenever and wherever they wanted. They would pull women out of their homes and rape them in the middle of the street during daytime as to show how much power and control they had over them. They also beat and murdered people in the middle of the street during daylight hours. They would then leave the murdered body in the streets like trash.

Years and years of this continual terror. Every home was victimized by this violent group of men. Every home except for one home. There was actually one home that these less-than human men would not touch. Year after year, visit after visit, they would harass and torment home after home. They would perform horrendous acts of violence inside and outside of homes within feet of the home they would not touch. Why? What was so different about that one home?

The video contained interviews with one of the adult women who lived in the house that was routinely spared. She said her parents taught their kids to educate themselves, become less dependent on others, and to continually develop their mind and brain. And that's exactly what they did. They were the only family to educate themselves at the local University in the entire section of where they lived. They were the only family that was not completely dependent on others. They developed their own intelligence (because they used school the right way) and their own self-worth. Their confidence was sky-high. I could even feel the women's self-built confidence oozing through the TV screen. Her family would become the confident, adaptable antelope that the crazed, indiscriminate lions would pass over.

Think about it, if a family or a community raises its young with too many oppressive rules and restrictions while discouraging continual learning, what type of confidence do we think those children will develop? Not much...and then they will become more dependent on others. That makes them easy targets to people who want to take advantage of them.

{5.26} How can that happen? How can one's confidence disengage a predator's possible attack? Before we get into that, of course, there are exceptions to most things. Here as well. Some people or animals with high levels of confidence can be controlled and manipulated but they are the exceptions for a reason. The vast majority of prey animals and Humans who are continually manipulated, controlled, or killed are the ones lacking confidence and the proper skills needed to defend themselves. There are less random predator-prey kills than we think. Predators (Humans or animals) stalk, observe, and learn about their prey before they attack. Why? It takes a lot of energy and time to attack or control someone else. Why waste time and energy on a confident, strong prey (victim) that can fight back equally or better than the attacker can? Most won't. They look for easy wins.

How can an animal predator figure out if a prey is weaker than them? The same way kids of our species do it. How do the bullies pick out the kids they want to harass and manipulate? Because many times, the bully has a victim picked out before even engaging with them.

There are at least three traits that virtually all species have used to analyze the danger or safety another individual may pose. The young of our species, before turning into biased, arrogant adults, use them as well. All or some of the three traits are used. Before a child figures out the complexities of our adult language, it uses these three traits extensively.

*The three non-verbal traits of which predator-prey interactions revolve around:*
*1. Body Posturing.*
*2. Eyes.*
*3. The Vibes (energy) between us.*

Predator-Prey interactions can be interpreted as many of our human-to-human relationships. Controlling, manipulative, selfish people act eerily similar to animal predators when evaluating their prey. Whether in dating, marriages, workplaces, or anywhere really, the approaches are strikingly similar. A controlling, manipulative man or woman will evaluate their potential partners before words are even spoken. They can read or feel an exploitable weakness in our eyes, in the way we hold our posture, the way we stand, the way we sit, or the vibes (energy) they get from us. Even though so many adults of our species continue to deny the existence and worthiness of emotions, feelings, and energy, they are all very wrong. There is an energy that exists between all living things. Just because we choose to ignore it and minimize it doesn't mean it's not there.

*It does not matter what our individual minds want us to believe or not, <u>energy</u> between all living things exists now and forever. It's invisible and easy to ignore but it is always there for us to use and be a part of. All living things have the ability to read their environment by allowing themselves to feel the type of energy that's around them. It happens every time we meet a new person or enter a new place. Without words, you can get a feeling about this person or place. On its most simplistic level, your feelings will go one of three ways. Either I feel safe with this person, I do not feel safe with this person, or I have a neutral feeling about this person. We have been doing this for millions of years. And this is just the surface of what we can feel. What are we capable of feeling? Can we feel if there is something wrong before something happens? Can we feel our way out of danger before it happens? Other animals have been doing this for a very long time so it's safe to assume that we have these capabilities as well. Too many adults tell too many children that feelings, energy, and emotions are useless wastes of time and these things make you weak. Those adults cannot be more wrong! This is a very damaging way to raise kids be-*

*cause the complete opposite is true. Using our millions-year-old highly developed sense of "being able to feel the energy in our environment" is a powerful ability many of us cast aside like trash.*

There is much to learn about the state of one's mind from a distance just by observing their eyes and body positioning. You can somewhat accurately assess their level of confidence and self-worth. The lower the confidence, the less the body posturing would be; lowered shoulders, drooping head, not standing fully upright, having a hard time making eye contact. Just with this one trait, it gives predators an opening, animal or Human.

What about eyes? It's the same as posturing, yet deeper. Eyes give away a lot of information. Especially to predators. Just look at a group of people...into their eyes. Some show high levels of confidence. Others show low levels of confidence through their eyes.

How can confidence change the look in our eyes? Some of it can be explained by the dilation and the constriction of the pupil, but overall long-term eye change occurs much deeper. The pupil is the opening into our eyes that allows light to enter. But what's around the pupil is more intriguing. The iris. The iris is the colored portion of the eye. It's made up of nerve fibers, which allows it to send and receive information. It connects and communicates extensively with our nervous system (brain and spinal cord). Interestingly enough, the iris of our eyes contain nerves that run through and communicate with every organ found throughout our body. When the organ is working at high, optimal levels, the iris reflects it. When an organ is underperforming, the iris reflects that as well.

Predators attack, use, manipulate, and control those who reflect weakness. The iris reveals this. Even when we can manage to hide our posturing flaws and stand up-right with false-confidence, our irises may tell a different story. Our iris is telling those around us the depth of our confidence. And it's coming from deep within our cells. It's hard as hell to hide this.

The iris is an extension of the nervous system that connects to other organs. *(When I try to solve problems, it really helps me to know what things are made up of and how they work, as well as what's responsible for controlling what I'm trying to figure out. Then it's like solving a puzzle after that; trying to fit together the pieces you have in front of you).* Organs are made up of tissues, which are made up of many different types of cells (skin cells, liver cells, lung cells). Cells, and what happens inside of them, is the key to our existence. Cells are like mini cities that perform countless jobs that keep us going. Our overall performance depends on their individual performance along with how they work and communicate with other cells around them. But what drives cells? ENERGY, ENERGY, ENERGY, ENERGY, ENERGY!

***On its most simplistic level, energy has a few options to energize whatever it is trying to energize:***
***1. It can give good, positive, life-enhancing energy.***
***2. It can be neutral and can have little or no effect at all.***
***3. It can give abnormal, life debilitating energy, which means it takes energy away over time.***

No matter what kind of energy it gives, if the same type of energy is continually and consistently fed into it, *that kind of energy* will continue to move up each link of life. Good, neutral, or bad energy that's created by and between those subatomic particles will have no choice but to send that type of energy upwards through atoms, molecules, cells, tissues, organs, and then us. The iris gives us some of this information about how our organs are behaving on a deep energy level. And then that reflects outwardly.

Think about the following: Which vibrational pattern would be the healthiest over a long period of time? Which would be the unhealthiest over a long period of time?

*A*

*B*

*C*

If our subatomic particles behave like **C** for years or decades, what do we think the performance would be like for our cells, organs, or us? What about *A* and **B**?

I would imagine **C** would eventually show up as multiple diseases in various organ systems along with behavioral and psychological problems. Our brains and everything else that makes up our physical bodies are controlled by the inner workings of our cells and subsequently the vibrational patterns of ENERGY given off by their subatomic particles. And **C** may be much more of an environmental and developmental problem rather than being born with bad genes.

Imagine throwing a rock into a body of water. Imagine that each wave and ripple of the water that comes off the center of where that rock entered the water is a wave or ripple of energy that comes from the center of a ball of energy deep within our cells. And every function in that cell is built upon and depends on that energy. What type of energy would allow our cells to work at high levels for sustained periods of time throughout our life? Weak, erratic, inconsistent, unpredictable waves of energy or consistent, strong, predictable waves of energy?

Both *B* and *C* are both going to cause problems somewhere in our bodies, minds, or brains eventually, but what is definitely going to cause problems is the inconsistency of those wave patterns. Because **B** only has inconsistency, its wave patterns are strong and life-enhancing, hence the non-wiggly lines. Wiggly lines show erratic energy behavior. But spaces between those waves or lines of energy shows inconsistency or consistency. **C** has two problems, while **B** has one problem. ***Even if something is erratic, if it's consistently erratic, at least you know how to prepare for it and possibly use it. If something is inconsistent, good or bad, it is a challenge to consistently rely on.***

For example, all of our biomes on Earth are based on the principle of consistency. How much rain an area receives is very important as is the time of year that it gets this amount of rain. However, when and what is the frequency of this rain? Does this area get rain consistently every week, every month, or inconsistently once or twice a year? Each area can receive the exact same amount of rain but if one area receives it inconsistently and randomly once or twice a year while the other receives it consistently and predictably, each biome's ecosystem will be built around *when* they receive the rain. The plants and animals may be much different because of the _consistency_ of the rainfall. This consistency is something they can build on. It's fundamental to the growth of entire ecosystems.

Even when we grow plants at home, you can see this pattern play out. I used to water my trees like this when I was stupid. I would water a certain amount for week one and again for week two...then forget for three weeks...then I would water a massive amount that wasn't close to the amount I used the first two weeks...then I would forget again and then try to compensate by flooding them again. The trees didn't die but they did not flourish either. They were more susceptible to disease and inconsistent growth as well. The amount of water wasn't the problem, it was my inconsistent watering and then me trying to overcompensate for my mistakes.

Even with kids, the same pattern plays out. Which kids would flourish more? Kids brought up by consistent parents or inconsistent parents? Would kids benefit more from parents spending quality time with them once a month for several hours (inconsistent flooding) or from parents spending quality time with them several minutes to hours every day (consistent watering)?

So even if **B** does not give off erratic waves like **C**, the inconsistent and wide spaces between those waves found in **B** make it very dangerous in the long-term.

*Most of these patterns (B and C) will not cause much damage to much of anything if it just lasts for a <u>short period</u> of time and is infrequent (too inconsistent to cause long-term damage). The long-term damage mostly comes from <u>long-term</u> vibrational patterns, both the inconsistent, and the erratic.*

*Good or bad, nearly anything done inconsistently every-now-and-then most likely will not cause any noticeable change in us. However, good or bad, mental or physical, anything done consistently over and over will eventually cause a noticeable change.*

Wave pattern *A* is the most desirable for us. It allows us and everything about us, physical or mental, to work at our absolute best. This is where the best of our health is, the best of our personalities, the highest functions of our brain, the best of our genetic functions, are found. **Short-term** occurrences in our cells like that of *B* and *C* are not a problem and most-likely won't cause many problems. Inconsistent and erratic **Long-term** vibrational patterns will, however. They can alter many things within us over a long period of time. Our cells (and us) and their long-term functions are highly dependent on what we consistently do over long periods of time, not over short time frames.

No matter what enters our minds, brains, bodies, it must be processed somehow, some way. And within that processing, the vibrational energy waves of our subatomic particles can and do change, which means we have enormous control over the energy deep within us that affects virtually every aspect of us and our life, the good and the bad.

Eating a few healthy meals per month has about the same effect as eating a few unhealthy meals per month, not much at all. Having a few positive thoughts per month surrounded by many more negative thoughts works very much the same way; it does not work. Inconsistent actions or thoughts are most likely not stored in our brains. Same goes if you are a person who has many positive, healthy thoughts throughout the month along with a few not so healthy, negative thoughts. The good thoughts will eventually overwrite the bad thoughts since the good thoughts have been given priority over the bad thoughts.

*We, and we alone, are responsible for programming how our bodies, our minds, and our brains react to and perceive the world around us.*

This relates to the iris of the eye. When we are mentally or physically injured, sick, diseased, or afraid, it shows up somewhere, in one or several places. Continual stress of any kind will eventually show up and express itself. It will most likely show up and exploit our weak points, whether those weak points are in our genetics, our physical body, or our mental or behavioral state. The irises of our eyes are one of those places that the stresses of our internal organs show up. No matter what we think we are portraying outwardly, our eyes may be telling others something different.

Make-up, clothes, hair, money, possessions, and put-on personalities cannot always mask what's bubbling underneath. One's eyes and one's energy reveals what one may be trying to hide inside.

*The energy deep within us controls virtually everything about us, who we are, and what we can become. We have control over much of that. No one else does unless we give it to them.*

We, each of us, have ultimate control over how our bodies, minds, and brains influence and guide our lives. We have ultimate control over the vibrational energy that controls virtually everything inside of us. There may be a few things we cannot control but there are far more parts of us that we can control. When we continually depend on others, we give up our control over ourselves and give it to them. The more diverse we become, the more adaptable we become, the more intelligent we become, the less others have control over us. We create our own energy, our own life. No one else does.

A great modern day example of evidence for how energy can change within us with as little as changing thoughts. Modern medical technology has finally gotten to the point where they are able to measure and record the vibrations created by cells deep within the human heart. This is not referring to blood pressure or heart rate, as it goes much deeper into the cells. They were able to monitor and record the vibrational wave patterns that the heart cells generated. The doctors were telling the patients different types of news. Some good, some not so good...and the vibrational patterns changed. When the patient felt good and excited with what they heard, the heart vibrations became more consistent and stronger. When the patient received news that was disturbing or sad, the vibrational frequency became less consistent, erratic, and weaker.

In the present day, we can now measure and record the vibrational patterns created by different atoms. Different atoms produce unique vibrational patterns. Diseased or injured cells produce unique vibrational patterns. And we also now know that these patterns can be altered by us, good or bad.

*We, you and I, have the ultimate control over all of this. We may not be able to control everything in our life, but we can control many more things that we were taught to believe. We can and do control our internal environment. We control how healthy we are, we control how capable we are, we control how intelligent we are, we control how free we are...*

{5.27} As you and I become more independent, confident, and free, we will encounter those of our species who will try to manipulate or take advantage of us. It helps if we can recognize the patterns of the narcissistic, controlling, selfish, manipulative people that live among us. The more we know, the better prepared we are. The better prepared we are, the less time we waste on people that do not deserve *our* time.

I have to keep reminding myself that some people will do anything in their power to keep their "Line" above my "Line." Many of their go-to moves evolved from this mindset and continually revolve around it. They will do whatever they can to keep you lower than them, less than them, unequal to them, and you can see it play out over and over, from high schools, to businesses, to families, and all the way up to our government leaders.

If they think someone is trying to move up and become their equal, something must be done to knock them back down.

*Oh, by the way, animals routinely do this in their own lives, trying to dominate others. If we Humans think we are above animals, many of our behaviors contradict that way of thinking.*

Let's go through a typical sequence of attacks and manipulations from people in our lives who want nothing more than to keep us lower than them. At this point I have to remind myself how tricky these people are because on the surface they know exactly what to say and how to act to get you to accept them and become comfortable with them. Then you are caught in their web of chaos. They got you. The sooner we recognize their patterns of manipulation, the sooner we can get away from these types of people.

<u>First</u> comes the insults, blaming, and verbal abuse. They will label us as something that is perceived as weak. Call us a nerd, a loser, hippie, sensitive, emotional, tree-hugger, nature-lover, etc. If that isn't enough, they will get others to follow their lead in bringing you down beneath them. They will also blame anything and everyone else for everything. They are never wrong in their heads.

If that doesn't work and we continue to rise to a level they are not comfortable with, they will try to keep us down in other ways. <u>Secondly</u>, they turn to rules and laws to keep us beneath them or use them to control us. If they are our bosses or our spouses, they will try to control us with laws and rules in the office or home or through the control of money. Many times they will not even follow these rules and laws, but demand that we do. "You can't cheat on me," they tell us, while they are cheating on us. These rules and laws are made for those beneath them, not for them, they will rationalize in their own minds. They believe they are above all rules and laws. They are usually heavily armed with an unlimited supply of excuses and contradictory reasoning. They are never wrong in their minds.

*They live by one simple rule: to keep others beneath and un-equal to them because they believe that they are more important than the rest of us.*

If degrading us doesn't work, if their rules and laws don't work to keep us where they want us, some then turn to the third option. That _third_ option is usually when it can get dangerous. Violence or harassment is used by some as another method to keep us below them as to control us. Remember the story of the city that was in constant attack from these groups of violent, corrupt men? Do you know when the only time they attacked that one house that they previously never touched was? It was when the family living in that house stood up to them and got the law on _their_ side. Those corrupt men attacked their house and their family. Fortunately, this family was intelligent enough to prepare for the attack. They knew and understood the patterns of these violent people. They were able to withstand the attacks.

You see this same scenario play out time and time again throughout the history of our species. Group A of people try to control Group B of people. Group A promises Group B that they can bring riches, happiness, and everything in the world to Group B. Group B believes Group A. Group A gets what it wants while slowly but surely eroding Group B's way of life. Group B becomes agitated and recognizes that Group A may not be so truthful. Group B stands up to Group A. Group A changes laws or rules or offers compromises that seem to help Group B on the surface. Group B is satisfied for a while. Then the same problems start to creep up again. Group B stands up to Group A again. Group A takes more rights away from Group B because they can. Group B backs down. Group A revels in another pointless "win." Group B stands up again. Group A responds with a higher level of disregard for Human rights. Higher levels of intimidation ensue; more lies, more assaults (verbal or physical), murder, excessive levels of harassment, etc, etc, etc...

Even in our relationships we see this same scenario play out when dealing with abusive, controlling, selfish, manipulative people. The controlling spouse ridicules and degrades their partner. Then isolates them from others. They manipulate other people to also look down on their partners. They then make up house and life rules that are designed to keep us under their control. If the victimized spouse decides to stand up to them, violence may ensue.

*Patterns...patterns...patterns. Our world is built upon patterns. Learn them and use them to make you stronger and more intelligent. For millions of years these same patterns have been playing out for us. If something is not working, recognize it, then change it!*

We see this grotesque behavior in administrative leaders all over the world in every nook and cranny of our societies. Even with our government leaders and lawmakers we see this play out continually. And these are the exact people that should be setting high standards for the young of our species. Yet, over and over, they fail miserably at that. Those who have power will do anything to keep that power even if it hurts everyone around them.

If one political party has power and the other political party is trying to take it, the same patterns emerge. The ones in power <u>first</u> pass blame, insult, name-call, ridicule, mock, and "label" the other party in an attempt to make them seem weak and less-than to the public. They attack them individually, then get others to join in the hate. <u>Secondly</u>, they change laws in their favor. They change laws to hurt others beneath them. They lie, they cheat, they manipulate as much as they can to retain power. They do not care about the average person. They do not care about helping others truly in need or care about people who are different from them. They only care about retaining power and keeping their "Line" above others.

*Like it or not, this is who we are as a species. We have been like this since the beginning. However, we are the one and only species that is capable of rising above this species-destroying behavior. We have to be the species that rises above what other animals cannot rise above. If we continue to demonstrate the same patterns of this animalistic behavior that has driven us for the last few million years, then we are no better than any other animal that has ever existed.*

*If we cannot get past this destructive behavior of inequality and obsessive control over other people's lives, this will most likely be one of the reasons for the end of our species.*

If we stand up to the people in our lives who are trying to control us, it can turn dangerous. They mostly don't have emotional attachments to much of anything, so that is an advantage to them. They are playing a different game than the rest of us. Emotions and feelings are critical to becoming a strong, confident, intelligent you but there are times they will get you in some trouble. When we get *too* emotionally attached to something or someone, it makes us vulnerable to attacks and manipulation by some people. Knowing this information beforehand is quite helpful when dealing with these types of Human mentalities.

The word "too" is really the problem. Too emotional is unbalanced and will make us weaker and easier to manipulate. "Too" much of anything is usually out of balance anyway. I try not to get too emotionally attached to something when dealing with people who "play the game" without emotional attachments to anything.

{5.28} If you are like me and are tired of what our species is and most likely what we have always been, there's some really good news.

Me and you don't have to be or do like the rest of our species. I would be willing to bet that 80–90% of all Humans who have ever existed have fallen into the same species traps that we continually set for ourselves. I sure did over and over again until I woke up! To avoid those repeated patterns that many of us continually fall for, it really helps to see our species for what we really are and to see that we do possess life-destructive traits. To recognize them is to be able to avoid them, while also exposing our many hidden gifts and talents.

I thoroughly believe we have the potential to solve all of our species' related problems. However, we keep falling into the same traps every generation of Humans before us has. By avoiding these traps, whether we are an individual, family, community, city, country, or culture, our potential to overcome anything is right in front of us, staring at us, waiting for us.

### _Common pitfalls our Species keeps falling into:_

- _Working <u>against</u> the Laws of Nature instead of with them._
- _Thinking of ourselves as greater than other people and greater than other species._
- _Hating, judging, isolating and not understanding others who are different from us._
- _Stopping continual learning while not pushing our brains and minds to higher levels._
- _Close our minds to any ideas that we don't agree with._
- _Depend heavily on others to take care of us and our needs._
- _Telling others what to do, who to be, and what to believe in._
- _Blaming others for our problems._
- _Not cleaning up after ourselves (physically, mentally, emotionally)._

You and I can go to places very few other Humans have ever been to, in our minds and in our brains. Besides working with the Laws of Nature, not against them, most of our problems are mental, not physical. I think if another advanced species from another planet would study our species for a while, they would come to the conclusion that we have a mental illness if we are not completely insane. We have been doing the same *wrong* things for much of our existence and haven't really changed our approach to anything. Except for building and inventing fancy, shiny new things, our species' mental approach to our existence has been pretty much the same as it's always been; power and control loaded with inequality followed by a lack of vision.

Even the way we think today is absurd. When do we ever just stop and figure out and fix the most basic, fundamental aspects of life as Humans on this planet? We should be able to master and eliminate many of the chronic, debilitating problems we currently have, like having clean water, clean air, high-quality parenting, equal Human rights, etc... Instead of trying to fix and solve, once and for all, the most basic, fundamental aspects of Human life on this planet, we put our efforts into colonizing another planet. Are we serious? We are failing miserably at taking care of this one planet. Before we decide to colonize another planet, maybe we should solve the following problems on ours first. We will no doubt have all the same exact problems there as we have here. You know...since we are the problem!

*1 - Air pollution*

*2 - Water pollution*

*3 - Poverty*

*4 - Homelessness*

*5 - Child abuse*

*6 - Inequality/hatred toward others who are different than us*

*7 - Preparing and educating our kids with real, usable knowledge and skills*
*8 - Lack of diversity of life*
*9 - Dirty, planet-polluting energy*
*10 - A neglected and abused Earth*

Can you imagine what life would be like on Earth if we finally put our differences aside and brought the brightest, most creative, most diverse minds together from all over the planet to put an end to poverty, pollution, inequality, homelessness, Human rights, abuse, destruction of our ecosystems, etc? What would life be like if we all were treated as equals, and we all had the same rights?

Will our species ever be able to see what life could be like on this planet if we did things opposite to the way we do things now? Are we not curious about what it could be? We are the first of any other time period of Humans that has ever reached this point of knowledge, understanding, communication, and technology. Are we not curious to what could be if we, if at least most of us, avoided those species' pitfalls? Life on this planet would be incredible!

*Because it's really quite simple to predict the next journey of our species if we keep falling headfirst into the same old pitfalls that most of our ancestors and us continually fall for. The next decade, the next century, the next 1000 years, or the next planet we live on, I bet I can predict what it will be like. Just like it is now. Lots of unnecessary, wasteful fighting, hating, manipulation by some of us toward others who are different, surrounded and masked by more shiny new inventions to take us into the future where we can't even solve our past.*

{5.29} I do not want this entire chapter to be about how our species is struggling. I do not want it to be all about our dark, destructive qualities. I want to end it with the incredible, life-enhancing traits that we possess. The traits that can fix any problem we face.

It has been challenging, disheartening, and an eye-opening experience for me as I learned about the destructive traits that our species possesses since the beginning of our time here. But the opposite is also true about our species and all the incredibly great traits we also possess. I found countless examples of how great we really are, or at least, we have the potential to be.

*I believe with everything that I have learned and observed, we have everything we need right now to fix any problem we face as a species. It all starts in our Human minds.*

We are the first of any species to gain this much knowledge and understanding of how intimately our world works. We are the first to be able to communicate with others anywhere on Earth within minutes. We possess the all-powerful, highly complex problem-solving Human brain. No one else does.

*If us as a species are capable of overcoming any obstacle, that means that you and I are as well.*

One of my favorite videos I ever watched was about two friends who planted over 10,000 trees together. That's a lot for any two people but these two friends had immense challenges. One was blind and the other had no legs. The blind friend carried his legless friend for several miles every day as they planted one tree at a time. The legless friend was the eyes for his blind friend. They had no vehicles and no equipment, just their will, desire, and passion to plant trees and to accomplish something worthwhile...something that had purpose.

Another favorite example of the potential we have is one I talked about earlier in the book about the Netherlands. On only 175 acres, they were able to grow enough high-quality, 95% chemical-free produce for their entire country. Again, on only 175 acres. They also had enough left over to export their produce all over the globe. They became one of the most profitable exporters of produce on the planet. And all was built in just 17 years. How did they do it? Pretty simple. There was a gathering of people from all over the country a few times a year to share ideas and information. What was unique about these people was that they were all different. Different ethnic groups, different educational backgrounds, different income levels, just different from one another. Very little judgment or bickering ensued because all people, along with their ideas, were accepted and discussed. When different types of people work together equally, incredible achievements are made.

*If we as a species can ever get past our own self-image, our arrogance, our hatred of others who are different, our obsession with controlling the lives of others, we would no doubt be an unstoppable force. We would be able to solve many of our species' chronic problems rather quickly. Most of our species' problems come down to treating others as unequal. That is the rotten "soil" we have created that infiltrates every aspect of our current existence. Change the "soil," change everything else.*

# Chapter 6

# The Young of Our Species

{6.1} When does it start? When do we begin to lose what we thought and believed life to be about? When does our life go from so promising and hopeful to...not that?

For the most part, most kids start off life with a lot of good, pure energy and much enjoyment for anything and everything. They are happy to be alive as they say...every day brings new, exciting adventures. Holidays are big, exciting events. Car rides to anywhere are similar to exploring outer space as a kid. Everything they look at is new to them. Every step is a new story, a new adventure...

Then, to many of us, sooner or later, something or someone changes us. We start to lose that excitement for life. As an adult, I have a much harder time maintaining the daily zest for the life that I had as a kid.

What happened? Why do so many of us change from happy kids to not-so-happy adults? Is this supposed to happen? Is there a specific point in life that changes the full-of-life kid to a half-of-life adult? Is there a pattern to this? Is it more genetic or environmental?

I asked myself, "Where should I start?" First off, I needed to be much more observant to what was happening around me. I started paying closer attention to people of all ages, trying to pinpoint a moment that the free child was starting to become not-so-free.

As usual, patterns emerged. Patterns started to show up when I slowed down, shut up, and observed unbiasedly without judgment or personal opinions.

*Our human brains learn much more deeply when they receive information that does not have our own personal bias attached to it.*

For me to be a better observer of others, I needed to understand myself a little better, especially as a kid. I needed to go back as far and deep as I could, and pull out as many memories as I could, the good and the bad. When was I happy? When was I not? What types of people, places, things, or situations would cause me to be happy or not happy? Were there patterns to these types of people, places, things, or situations that caused these feelings?

I was especially digging into my head holding the memories that I had prior to turning 12. Much of our adult personalities are created and developed during the time between birth to 12 or so years old. What happens in our lives between birth and 12 years old is by far one of the most important time periods in which the development of the brain and mind occurs. More on that later...

→→ ··◆· ·←←

*Side thought on living life or making decisions based on one or a small few inspirational quotes. As with most living things, variety and diversity reign king. There were some inspirational quotes that I used to live by. And not just quotes from books; many adults around me would repeat the same quotes as if they were giving me the wisest information that ever was. I would live by these supposedly great ideas because I trusted the adults around me. I never thought about the deep underlying meaning of any of them, just thought they must work because adults, who I trusted, are telling me they do it. Also, some of this life advice has been given for thousands of years. So they must work, right? At least that's what I was telling myself. I sure wasn't intelligent or confident enough to question what adults were telling me. Even through most of my adulthood, I still wasn't intelligent or courageous enough to question any kind of advice given, good or bad.*

*So, I would take an inspirational life-message like, "Live in the now," and never question it. I was told by many older and supposedly wiser adults than me to "forget the past, live in the present." As I got older, I started to question more, even question ideas from the greatest minds of our species' history.*

*My first question was this: why would I limit information that could help me, make me smarter, make me stronger and more confident? My past, especially my childhood, holds so many answers and reasons for my adult life and my adult decisions. Why would I forget the past? Our Human brains thrive and grow with diversity and a variety of information. Living my life strictly under one or a very few ideas or beliefs is not variety...or smart...at all. Life can be quite difficult and challenging at times. I wanted to give myself as many options as I could during these times as a way to get out and not get stuck. The more I restricted certain types of information from entering my brain, the more I started to remove my variety of options. I was boxing myself in. Why would I only live in the present? I want as much information as I can get about my past, my present, and my future. I just don't get too emotional when dealing with past and future events. Stressing and worrying about past events brings on depression, while worrying about future events brings on anxiety. Avoid these (depression and worrying) by not getting emotionally attached to past and future events. We can still get valuable information without getting emotionally attached.*

{6.2} Besides digging up my childhood, which takes time, I decided I needed to further simplify my approach. What about taking Humans out of it for a bit? What about learning from animals again? Young animals tend to play and not have much stress compared to the older animals. Similar to us. Most of us are playful and carefree before our 20s. And then, time and time again, generation after generation, a massive up-swelling of more unhappy adults. Why do we have so many happy children becoming so many unhappy adults?

Maybe all the adult animals are all very stressed and frustrated with life but can't verbalize it like we can. Maybe that's just the way things are? Nope, that's stupid. I see and meet happy adults all the time. It can't be an animal thing, right? It's not, because we as Humans, unlike animals, have the ability to figure out what is wrong with us and fix it.

**We should have the ability to control, at this point in our existence, some or all of our deeply ingrained natural animalistic behaviors without them controlling us.**

*An older male coyote, when sexually excited, may force himself onto a younger, smaller female coyote. When in this excited state, the male coyote has an almost uncontrollable urge to breed, with little regard to what happens next or how this type of action may affect his or her life later on. Us as Humans, have all the same desires and urges (like sex) as the animals around us have. But we are the one species that should be able to control our deep animalistic behaviors that cause harm to ourselves or others in the long run. Virtually all of our Human behaviors are found throughout the animal kingdom. We individually choose if they take us down or lift us up.*

Observing animal behaviors as my own uncovered more patterns within me. Animal adult behaviors would change for the better when certain things happened. I bet these will sound familiar...

- **Consistent reliable food supply.**
- **Consistent reliable security (home).**
- **Strong ecosystems (communities) around them.**

Yes, domestic and wild animals (adults and their young) displayed signs of low stress and high comfortability when their basic needs of life were *consistently* met.

{6.3} I often play the "What If" game in my head to expand my perceived perception of reality. I was often told by many adults in my life to not ask "What if?" because it was a pointless and dangerous question to ask. And as usual, those adults were wrong and short-sighted. Asking "What if?" allows our brains to visualize new paths, new alternatives, before actually going through with it. Asking "What if?" allows us to make better short-term decisions to enhance our long-term life. This allowed expansion and openness in my mind, which allowed for expansion and openness in my brain. I again questioned the advice of many adults I have come across.

What if we, as Humans, are just like animals and all the other living things with how we interact with our environment? What if we, as

Humans, are no greater in importance than all other living things on Earth? What if we are just the next living thing "Up?" Whether we were created by a Creator or we were not created by a Creator, the underlying situation we are in remains the same; we and all living things have grown and evolved together for a very long time on this planet.

If we are built like other animals, we can learn much about ourselves from them, especially our strengths and weaknesses as a species.

*"No matter what my mind wants to tell me what to think, I will allow my brain to absorb this new information, as unbiasedly as I can," is what I tell myself repeatedly with any new information.*

How would I navigate through life without being able to verbally express myself though? How would I know if someone was trying to help me, scam me, or hurt me if I can't verbally communicate with them? Animals can and do, all day every day. They don't need to talk or hear each other to know what's going on. We each, as Humans, have the ability to feel what's around us, much like other animals do.

The same insecurities and securities that drive our everyday lives are very similar to all other living things and their insecurities. All living things perform better in their environment when all their core, fundamental needs are met. Consistent resources in a consistently secure environment will produce the best in any species. We are no different. When our securities are threatened, we respond like any other living thing would. We try to get our security back. The best a species has to offer is seen when it has its basic, fundamental securities met. Consistent and reliable food, water, resources (income), community, and a safe, secure home. All ecosystems respond in a highly positive way when these basic, fundamental aspects of life are met consistently and reliably.

We see the worst in a species when these needs are inconsistent or unreliably met. It does not matter who or what you are, if you are a living thing and you live in an inconsistent, unreliable environment that pushes you to your limits, some of your greatest weaknesses (i.e. genetically, physically, mentally, behaviorally, hormonally, epigenetically, developmentally, etc.) will be expressed over and over. Constant ssdtress (internal and external) brings out the worst of us while unstressed brings out the best.

But what about insecurities that are not even within the living world? Stresses that we make up? Man-made stresses, like money. One of my insecurities is lack of money. Why is that? Money is not a real living, breathing thing; it has been made up by man. It only exists because of our species.

Then why is it such a driving force in our lives? Since our species invented it, it should not bring us stress and insecurity. But it does bring us lots of stress and insecurity. It also gives us a false sense of security since it's not a real living thing.

*Why am I happier when I have money and why am I unhappier when I don't have it? That makes zero sense to me. Something that is not living, breathing, bleeding, or breeding controls so many of my life-decisions and also not so good for my stress levels. Why?*

Security. Easy enough. If I have money, then I have all the other necessities and securities taken care of. I can relax, right? I wish. False or fake securities have wildly fluctuating not-so-good ups and downs while true, real-life securities have more stable and not-too-bad ups and downs.

If money was a true security for Humans, damn near all the people with enough money to live comfortably and feel secure, should be living happy, healthy, content, peaceful, well-balanced lives...right?

That's kind of how it works with all other living things that have their securities taken care of. Not so much with us and our money though. We're the only species that deals with money. We're the only species that depends on it, not biologically, but in present day society, as a way of life. If all other species get their real-world securities from something that isn't money, I'm betting our true securities and our key to a balanced, badass, very free life is not through money.

{6.4} Let's walk through a few different scenarios. We'll try to guess which one would flourish the most throughout its entire life.

### Scenario 1:

_Fawn A (Baby deer)_

_1. Born in an area where food sources are scattered and far from cover._

_2. Sparse, not-too-thick security and cover._

_3. No other family members besides mom._

_4. An abundance of predators._

_5. Imbalance of other animals living and feeding in the same areas (overpopulation of some species and under-population for others)._

**OR...**

_Fawn B (Baby deer)_

_1. Born in an area where food sources are close to safe, thick from cover._

_2. Thick cover, nearly impenetrable security._

_3. A diverse family unit with mom, aunts, cousins, brothers, and sisters_

_4. Balanced number of predators._

*5. A good balance of other animals living and feeding in different and diverse areas.*

### Scenario 2:

*Seed A (Plant embryo)*

*1. Planted earlier/later than the appropriate time of the year.*

*2. Planted with many other seedsaround it, competing with it.*

*3. Planted in soil that is out of balance.Too many are too few nutrients.*

*4. Planted in soil that is inconsistently fed and watered.*

*5. Allowed to grow in soil that is too firm for the roots to grow deep.*

**OR...**

*Seed B (Plant embryo)*

*1. Planted right around the appropriate time of the year.*

*2. Planted with few seeds around it.*

*3. Planted in soil that is nutrient balanced.*

*4. Planted in a soil that is consistently fed and watered.*

*5. Allowed to grow in soil that is just loose enough to all allow the roots to grow and access more areas.*

### Scenario 3:

*Our Gut Bacteria A*

*1. Many of them competing for space and food.*

*2. Inconsistent food.*

*3. Lower quality food.*

*4. Many "predators" killing them; chemicals in the gut, toxins, long-term low quality foods and liquids.*

*5. Poor unreliable, inconsistent living conditions.*

**OR...**

*Our Gut Bacteria B*

1. *A balanced amount that has its own space and food.*
2. *Consistent food.*
3. *Higher-quality food.*
4. *Not many "predators" entering the gut to cause negative effects.*
5. *Consistent, reliable living conditions.*

We get the point. No matter what the living thing is, a consistent, reliable, safe, secure environment produces the best. Diverse, adaptable, strong, dependable surroundings are essential to building better, stronger, more adaptable plants, bacteria, animals, and of course then, us. Strong surroundings influence those within those surroundings. When too many plants are planted in a small area with limited resources, then what happens? Stress sets in with each of those individual plants. Their organ systems (leaves, stems, roots) are starting to become less efficient and less productive. Their immune systems weaken. They grow less. They produce less. If the factor that is causing the stress continues, then the plant will not be able to reach its potential. As its growth and immune system slows, diseases set in. It bears less fruit. But what happens when we remove the stressors, especially when young? The weeds around the plant, competing for resources are removed. The plant's own roots now have zero competition when trying to pull nutrients out of the soil. The plant now has its own personal space and room to grow and be free to reach its potential. Of course, a consistent, reliable, high-quality food source would then be its next security to obtain. If the competing weeds are removed and the plant receives a consistent high-quality food source, the plant can then focus its energy on other things, like growing, developing, and reproducing.

The plant now gets taller, the immune system gets stronger; the plant now gets fewer diseases. It recovers faster. Plant also produces more than it's ever produced. Its needs were met.

*Children have to be the same, right? What I have to keep telling myself is, "No matter what my Human mind wants me to believe, the Laws of Nature (physics, chemistry, biology, etc.) ARE THE SAME IN ALL LIVING THINGS AND HAVE BEEN AROUND FOR BILLIONS OF YEARS! I must adapt to them, not the other way around."*

How then do we suppose we "remove the weeds" from the environment around our children? As with plants, not all plants growing around them are life-sucking weeds, some of those perceived "weeds" are beneficial to the growth of the plant. So, it's important to evaluate which "weeds" help or hurt.

Problem (i.e. negative energy) weeds were using energy from the soil that the plant could have been using, while also taking physical space away from the roots of the plant. It was physically crowding its space while also taking away usable energy. It was crowding its space, not allowing it to be free and grow.

{6.5} Removing the weeds gave the plant its own free space. Space to grow and be free. For us, it's creating our own personal space and time to allow for personal and intellectual growth. For Human children to have the chance to reach their full potential, they need and deserve the right to have their own personal free space to grow and develop.

For the most part, the "weeds" that need to be removed for the benefit of the child, are the adults' negative energies in that child's life that continually drain the positive energy and personal freedom of that child. I do not mean to physically separate the child from the adult (of course, in some cases, removal is helpful). The weeds that suck the energy from a growing, developing child are not the physical body of the adult, they are the words, actions, and emotions (vibrational frequencies) of the adults.

Our words, actions, and energies as adults influencing our children can alter their developmental environment in very good or very bad ways. Time and time again, situation after situation, era after era, generation after generation, it continues to happen. Each generation of adults "weeds" their own beliefs and ideologies into that generations' kids, with little to no regard to what or how the children may think or feel about it, or eventually respond or react to it.

How many times have we heard an adult say, "This is the way it's gonna be, we've always done it this way. I don't need your opinion, just do like I say!" That behavior is a good weed to pull. That type of "weed" will suck out all kinds of good energy from the "soil" around our kids. And for what? So us adults who cannot adapt can have it our way?

It doesn't take much to start the young neurological pathways (the paths that allow our brain and spinal cord to communicate with everything in and on us) in the young of our species down the wrong path.

**Our "weeds" as adults, that we should be removing, are the strict, suppressive beliefs and ideas that we put onto our kids.**

The "weeds" are life-inhibiting to our children over the course of their life. This selfish type of adult behavior is one of the major "weeds" preventing our children from reaching their full potential. And if that selfish, my-needs-first adult behavior is a consistent type of behavior throughout the child's developmental period, the child's brain will be wired incorrectly. And that is the adult's fault, not the child's.

**The parents of a child have an incredible amount of influence on the development of their own child's brain and mind.**

We, as adults, should strive to teach children as many skills as we can and *let them decide* which choices to make and what to believe in and what not to believe in. By pushing our ideas and beliefs onto them, we are taking their personal freedom away from them, which does not allow them to see everything as it is. When personal space and freedom are taken away from virtually any living thing, that living thing, in virtually all scenarios, does not and cannot reach its full potential. In many cases, one will fight like hell to gain or preserve its freedom.

In almost all Human relationships, the breaking point, or at least the turning point, is when one feels a loss of personal freedom or a feeling of inequality. When one tries to invade or take away another's personal space or freedom, friction ensues.

*The lightbulb for this type of understanding completely bursted when something fascinating happened between me and my family's dog. This is how it played out:*

*I had my own two dogs that I had owned and lived with since they were puppies. I was very close with them. I spent a lot of time with them as we shared a special bond. Then as life goes by, living situations eventually changed and some of my family members moved in with me, along with their pets.*

I would make it a point to pet and play with all dogs present, mine or not. After a year or so, I began to notice a difference in behavior toward me when comparing my dogs to my family's dogs. I immediately thought that was normal because mine grew up with me and were more comfortable with me than the other dogs. So this must be a natural reaction by the dogs I thought.

Of course, I wasn't satisfied with that answer. What if it was something that I was doing differently between the dogs that I was unaware of while the dogs were picking it up? I felt like I was petting them the same and giving them the same amount of attention, but something still did not seem right. Was I wrong?

So, one day I decided to go up to one of the dogs that was not mine, that didn't grow up with me, but has been living with me for over a year at this point. He was an elderly dog who was found lost and most likely lived in several homes. He was naturally a really nice, calm, laid-back dog. But he didn't express the same excitement for life my dogs seemed to possess. So, I put myself in his place. What if I was him, as a dog, who "has been moved to yet another house after being lost for who knows how long. And then when I get here, the owner (me) is a really nice guy who pets me and stuff, but definitely treats me differently than his own dogs"?

My next immediate thought jumped to how stepchildren might feel living in a new home with a new family. Many families naturally treat their own a little better than those who are not their own. We all do it. It's natural. But it's not okay. It can be quite damaging to those kids forced into those types of relationships.

I had to see if I could do that for my family's dog. Could I show him that he was just as important to me as my dogs were? Immediately my mind went to finding everything I liked better about my dogs in trying to justify why I treated them differently. Then I asked myself, "What if

I owned my family's dogs and they owned my dogs from birth? Would I still make the same justifications that I just made? Am I treating them unequally because I'm more comfortable with the ones I've been living with longer and it really has nothing to do with them?"

I then walked up to my family's dog. I bent down and started to pet him and give him more attention than I normally gave him... Nothing happened. I gave him more time and more petting... Nothing really any different happened. He would walk away from me the same way he always did.

I thought more and deeper... What am I missing? I thought he was an animal. Animals, as well as our own children, are really good at one thing... Feeling their way through fake or false adult actions and words that we portray toward them.

That was it! He was feeling through what I was trying to artificially portray. I thought by just spending a certain amount of time with him with just the right amount of attention would satisfy the inequality he felt living here. He felt right through that BS I was trying to pass over him. He was right. Because as I was spending time petting him and giving him more attention than I ever gave him before, I was thinking about everything else I had to do in my life while my head was somewhere else, not with him. He nailed me.

So, I went back to him again and did something different. I eliminated everything in my head. I stopped thinking about my schedule, my to-do list, my life, everything... I just focused on him. I petted him for several more minutes. I let go of all of my stresses and all of my to-do lists. I let go of everything. My breathing calmed. My heart rate was peaceful.

When I stopped petting him, he immediately started jumping up and down over and over, constantly wagging his tail. He looked like a young dog again. I couldn't believe it. I could not believe the change in him *when I gave him full, real, equal attention. He now runs up to me when he sees me with his tail wagging. And I now treat him as one of my own.*

It's quite easy to be successful at Human relationships. If we allow the other person in the relationship—and it does not matter what kind of relationship we have with them—to be themselves without judgment and treat them as equals, we will find success. It's damn near that easy. **The moment we start to try to change people into what we think they should be or treat them as less than us, problems will show up and never leave.**

{6.6} Since I've been writing this book and thinking about our species' roles as adults preparing the young of our species for life's challenges, a few thoughts have continually shown up. One of those thoughts that shows up consistently during arguments with myself is about us creating barriers in the brains of the children that we are supposed to be breaking down. Not all of us adults, but many, way too many, fail miserably when it comes to allowing children to make their own decisions about their own life.

Obviously, adults should make some decisions for the children under their influence but for the most part; highly successful children and adults pretty much all were developed from similar environments. Environments that did not restrict freedom of thought and choices continually produced successful people of all ages. Environments that enhanced the mind and brain, not restricted it. Environments surrounding children with diversity of thought will always dominate environments that restrict diversity of thought. These environments that develop and create our children are not guided by money, government, or community status. We don't need money, governments, or expensive schools to produce successful children. We need to get out of the way of the developing child's brain. As adults responsible for the development of our next generation, we should allow for a high diversity of unbiased information to enter their brains.

Our Human brains, like computers and every other living thing that is trying to learn from its environment, is only as intelligent as the diversity of information, ideas, or programs that are allowed to enter it. Then, if given enough time to work on and deeply connect the newly acquired diverse information, advanced levels of intelligence and highly complex problem-solving capabilities start to develop.

*It's quite difficult to imagine a scenario where a restrictive mind and brain (not open to new ideas or continual learning) would out-perform a wide-open mind and brain (open to continual learning of old and new things) in any scenario in any aspect of life.*

I would imagine it is physiologically impossible for a Human brain to become an intelligent, problem-solving brain if the mind around that brain blocks new information and new ideas from entering it. Which computer do we think would be able to outperform and be a better problem-solver? A computer with 30 different programs or a computer with six nearly identical programs?

We have zero rights as adults to restrict the type of information that enters our children's brains based on our own beliefs and ideas. **I am not talking about restricting kids from inappropriate adult content. That's different from this.**

Did our parents have the right to withhold or dismiss information from us? Especially if that information did not agree with their opinions, beliefs, and their ideologies? NO, THEY DID NOT!

On the most simplistic level of how the most fundamental physiological workings of the brain operate; withholding, dismissing, hiding, or altering information that we as adults give to our children will absolutely make their brains less intelligent and a not-so-good problem solver. In turn, later in life, time and time again, generation after generation, they then have trouble as an adult when it comes to fixing their own problems.

**We, as adults, are directly to blame or praise when it comes to the failures or successes of our children.**

*I use the following phrasing when talking to kids now (whether it is a belief or thought I have): "Well, since you asked, I'll tell you what I think about that. But before I tell you what I think and believe about what you asked, let me start with this. What I'm about to tell you are my beliefs and thoughts based on my experiences through my life. These are my thoughts, but they don't have to be yours. I highly encourage you to explore many different types of beliefs and ideas on this question. This is just the way I see it; you may see it completely different.*

{6.7} Those of us who are restricting freedom of thinking and learning to a child, we are doing immense harm to them, which can and will affect them every day of their life until their death. If we give our kids six mostly similar thoughts and beliefs to navigate through life with, how successful can they really be? How many problems do we think those kids could solve on their own

More times than not, this is the turning point in a child's life, when a child's freedom of thought and expression is taken away. Us adults continually give out instructions to children on how to live, who to be, what to do, and how to do it. And we tend to give out these life-instructions with very few other options. What do we think will happen to the following neighborhoods over the course of several decades?

## Neighborhood A

- _2_ out of every _10_ houses:

1. Live under a restricted, close-minded environment.
2. Certain types of information from certain types of people are not allowed.
3. Separates from and looks down upon those who are different.
4. Mocks and ridicules those who learn and try to better themselves.

   **OR...**

## Neighborhood B

- _8_ out of every _10_ houses:

1. live under a restricted, close-minded environment.
2. Certain types of information from certain types of people are not allowed.
3. Separates from and looks down upon those who are different.
4. Mocks and ridicules those who learn and try to better themselves.

Which neighborhood do we think will produce more successful children-turned-adults 10, 20, 30 years down the road? Which city, state, culture, country, and species would produce more successful adults?

The children of this generation are similar to our gut bacteria and the soil in our forests and gardens; with our young being the essential foundation that supports us and gives us many benefits later on down the road when we are older as we need their support and problem-solving abilities.

Even when talking just about us (our species) and our gut bacteria, there is a strong connection between them and our brain and how it functions. There is a strong neural (brain) connection with our digestive system, mainly our lower portion, our colon (large intestine). That's where most of our bacteria live. Several pounds of us are made up of microscopic bacteria. These are crazy important to our existence. Our brain and gut bacteria talk and communicate with each other a lot. The brain can give information to the digestive tract just as it can give information to the brain. The gut is often referred to as the second brain.

Which gut do we think would communicate better with the brain? Which gut do we think would be able to digest and utilize the energy from food better? Which gut do we think would have a strong immune response?

### Gut A

1. Houses a few types of bacteria.
2. Bacteria that have been exposed to a <u>low</u> variety of microorganisms entering the digestive tract, from a diet that is too processed, far from its natural state.
3. Exposed to a low variety of foods.
**OR...**

### Gut B

1. Houses many different types of bacteria.
2. Bacteria that have been exposed to a <u>high</u> variety of microorganisms entering the digestive tract from a diet that is close to its natural state.
3. Exposed to a high variety of foods.

As with most things in nature, high diversity usually outweighs low diversity. A population of virtually anything is stronger with a high diversity of genetics (DNA), as well as a population with a high diversity of physical differences. Any brain that contains a high diversity of unbiased information is stronger and more capable than a brain receiving low diversity of information. Hence, the health, vigor, and diversity of our gut bacteria will no doubt have unlimited health benefits for us now and later.

Same with forest and garden soil. If the soil (as well as our gut bacteria) *consistently* receives high quality food and has a healthy, balanced environment around it, they will both continually solve problems for us without us even knowing.

If a plant receives an abundance of nutrients consistently and is not living in a toxic environment, the plant has the ability to strengthen itself and defend itself from attacks. If the soil is well-balanced and full of life and has good communication and contact with the roots of the plant, it can not only defend itself, it can also send signals to its neighbors, warning them of the possible attack. Can it defend against anything? No, but the plant can withstand more than a plant in a poorer, restrictive environment. And even if it gets sick, diseased, or attacked, its response and recovery time is much quicker.

Should be the same for our gut bacteria, right? If they live in a well-balanced, highly diversified, healthy environment, they should be providing us countless benefits that we may not even be aware of, right? Up to 80% of our immune system is made up of gut bacteria. Probably important to take care of them if we want to live a longer, healthier life.

{6.8} A simple look at common patterns within living systems.

**_Unhealthy soil_** = *unhealthier plants* = *more disease, more infections, more bad bugs* → **_More problems later_**

**_Healthier soil_** = *healthier plants* = *less disease, fewer infections, fewer bad bugs* → **_Fewer problems later_**

**_Unhealthy Gut bacteria_** = *unhealthy person* = *more digestive problems/lowered immune system/more disease* → **_More health problems later on._**

**_Healthy Gut bacteria_** = *healthier person* = *fewer digestive problems/healthy immune system/less disease* → **_Fewer health problems later on._**

To me, these two analogies can be compared to the young of our species in this generation, or the children of any generation. The young of any Human generation are extraordinarily similar to gut bacteria, forests, and garden soils with regards to how they can handle, respond, and recover from short-term and long-term stresses that they will no doubt encounter throughout their lives.

The adults of any generation are the after-effects of the environment that they as children were exposed to repeatedly and consistently. Our minds, brains, personalities, strengths, and weaknesses are not built from a few random events in our lives but through repeated, consistent events; good, bad, and/or neutral.

What do we think would be "good soil" for the surrounding environment of a kid? It would be quite surprising if it wouldn't stick to the very common patterns that all living things in the natural world seem to adhere to.

- ***Unbalanced Environment*** = *Poor Environment* = *Unhealthy Individuals* → ***More problems later.***

- ***Balanced Environment*** = *Healthy Environment* = *Healthy Individuals* → ***Fewer problems later.***

- *Fearful/Restrictive/**Unbalanced**/Low Diversity Environment* = *Unhealthy Child* → ***More problems later.***

- *Confident/Open/**Balanced**/High Diverse Environment* = *Healthy Child* → ***Fewer problems later.***

***When we, as adults, create an unbalanced, unhealthy environment for our young, we are to blame for their problems created later, not them. We set up their fundamental foundation wrong.***

{6.9} Many times at home, an unhealthy, unbalanced environment will begin creating problems in the short-term that may go unnoticed while becoming much bigger problems in the long-term. How are problems solved then? Because all problems can be solved, right?

At least at a minimum, we should give ourselves many options to solve our problems. Adults, children, and any other living thing feels trapped when only given a few options or choices. Without options is without hope. Without hope is without much else. Hope gives purpose to one's life. If one has purpose, life decisions start to change, and usually for the better. A trapped child or anybody of any age that feels trapped in any situation will most likely have a natural reaction to get out. But if our options are limited because of our environment, we have less ability to get out of these problems (traps). **Hence, strict,**

**restrictive, close-minded parents who intentionally or unintentionally withhold information from their kids because of their own beliefs and ideologies are trapping their own kids into corners with very few options.**

Is it the same for adults as well? Do we feel a loss of self when our freedom of thought is being taken away? Does our perspective of life change when we start to lose the freedom we once had as a child? Do we feel trapped when our once-free world becomes entangled and seemingly trapped in life's oh-so-typical and not-so-free problems?

Forcing ourselves and the children we have influence over to be restricted to certain narrow points of view are Human-made traps. As for children, we adults are blocking their ability to build their own brain and mind with new, old, and different ideas. We are blocking their ability to build massive, complex, problem-solving neural networks deep throughout their brains. Any brain that is loaded with a high diversity of new and old ideas rarely feels trapped or a loss of freedom. Any brain that is NOT loaded with a diversity of ideas can frequently feel trapped and isolated. A brain with a low variety of ideas and options can get frustrated easily since it lacks the ability to get out of its own problems.

*When I force or encourage a child that I have influence over to believe my perspectives as the only option, I'm not really allowing the child the freedom of personal choice. That's a loss of freedom. A loss of freedom can be crushing to any of us, especially a child. I have no rights as an adult to directly or indirectly force my beliefs or perspectives on any child.*

By forcing our beliefs, ideologies, and opinions onto them, we are doing much harm to them now and in the future. We are also going to cause problems for ourselves later in life when these kids grow up into adults. Guess what kind of adults these kids will become; those kids that had restricted, distorted views of life with limited-options in their environments? They may depend heavily on us as we become older and less capable. = "More problems later."

*It takes courage and confidence in oneself as a parent or as an adult role model to stand aside and let those children under our influence choose as they can freely choose. Many of us automatically tell others what to do, who to be, rather than just letting them be. Let them try, let them fail, let them compete and complete, let them succeed. The most successful Humans ever to exist have figured this out and lived by this simple yet effective perspective of raising and preparing their own kids for life's challenges.*

{6.10} Adults who live a restricted, present life-only life, with little connection to their past or their future, tend to live in fear and lack real self-confidence. Adults who lack self-confidence and long-term vision will continually struggle with change. Restricted, highly controlled environments make us feel safe and secure. It makes us feel like we are doing better than others. We fight to keep it, even if it causes long-term harm to us or our family. In reality, however, restricted, highly controlled environments limit our options. Limited options usually don't offer much help when life throws you some challenges, especially when we are really low.

As with anything in life, we will begin to feel trapped and less free when our options run thin. However, if we Humans are brought up in environments that consistently allows our brains and minds to continually develop and explore different options, we will eventually acquire a limitless supply of options to overcome any of life's challenges.

For now and forever, it's the responsibility of the adults of the present generation to equip the young of the next generation with many options to go along with many usable skills. We do not, as adults, have the right to limit options we hand down to our kids. We should not remove their right to gain valuable knowledge that could benefit their lives. We are setting them up for failure when we restrict them.

If we want to go down as the smartest species ever, it starts with how we prepare our own young. We cannot and will not be able to accomplish much as a species if we fail to develop our own.

And once again, we have all the tools and knowledge we need right now to help our kids prosper no matter what challenges they may face.

*Final Thoughts...*

As this may have not been the fondest look at our species, it may be one of the truest. We have everything we need right now to solve all of our problems. We can become one of the greatest advanced species that the universe has ever seen, or we can go down as the species that gave up this incredibly rare opportunity that we have been given. Can we get out of our own way and become one of the most dominant species ever throughout the universe? Only we decide that...

See you on the other side of the Human Mind...

**Tips and Strategies to becoming a highly successful Human on Planet Earth:**

1. Learn the Laws of the Universe.

2. Live according to the Laws of the Universe.

3. Eliminate hate of others.

4. Eliminate judgment of others.

5. Treat others as equals.

6. Judge and critique yourself as you would judge and critique others.

7. Develop full accountability of your life problems; stop blaming others for your life circumstances.

8. Learn a variety of useful skills.

9. Develop a diverse learning brain and mind that is highly adaptable.

10. Develop a deep connection with our Planet.

Milton Keynes UK
Ingram Content Group UK Ltd.
UKHW042256170324
439575UK00004B/262